55 Hikes in™
CENTRAL
WASHINGTON

55 Hikes in™
CENTRAL
WASHINGTON

Ira Spring
and
Harvey Manning

Second Edition

THE
MOUNTAINEERS

Published by
The Mountaineers
1001 SW Klickitat Way, Suite 201
Seattle, Washington 98134

First edition 1990. Second edition: first printing 1997, second printing 1999

Published simultaneously in Great Britain by Cordee, 3a DeMontfort Street, Leicester, England, LE1 7HD

Manufactured in the United States of America

Edited by Dana Fos
Maps and book layout by Gray Mouse Graphics
Photographs by Harvey Manning: pages 57, 59, 61, 62, 64, 65, 68, 77, 82, 85, 86, 88, 90, 159. All others by Bob & Ira Spring.
Cover and book design by The Mountaineers Books

Cover photograph: *Frenchman Coulee, Quincy Wildlife Recreation Area* © Bob and Ira Spring *(Hike 38)*
Frontispiece: *Deep Lake, Sun Lakes State Park (Hike 45)*

Library of Congress Cataloging-in-Publication Data
Spring, Ira.
  55 Hikes in central Washington / Ira Spring and Harvey Manning.—[2nd ed.]
     p.   cm.
  Includes bibliographical references.
  ISBN 0-89886-510-7
  1. Hiking—Washington (State)—Guidebooks. 2. Mountaineering—
Washington (State)—Guidebooks. 3. Washington (State)—Guidebooks.
I. Manning, Harvey. II. Title.
GV199.42.W2S645   1997
796.5'09797'5—dc21   96-48077
                                                           CIP

CONTENTS

Introduction 9

Southern State 35

1. Lyle-to-Goldendale Rails-to-Trails: Swale Canyon 36
2. Cherry Orchard Trail 38
3. Horsethief Lake State Park 39
4. Crow Butte 42
5. Two Sisters (Two Captains) Rocks 44
6. Juniper Dunes Wilderness 46
7. Tucannon River 48
8. Chief Old Bones 50
9. Palouse Falls 51
10. Pasco–Fish Lake–Spokane Rails-to-Trails 53

Yakima Area 57

11. Sedge Ridge 58
12. Darling (Darland) Mountain 61
13. Blue Slide Lookout 63
14. Narrow Neck Gap 66
15. Conrad Meadows 68
16. Cowiche Canyon Conservancy 70
17. Bear Canyon 71
18. Naches River–Cougar Canyon 73
19. Cleman Mountain 75

Umtanum East 77

20. Yakima River View 78
21. Umtanum Canyon 80
22. Yakima Rim Skyline Trail 81

Umtanum West 93

23. Hardy Canyon 94
24. Black Canyon–Umtanum Ridge Crest 96
25. Audubon Camp 98
26. Manastash Ridge 100
27. West Manastash Ridge 102

Potholes 105

28. Winchester Wasteway 106
29. Potholes Island Hideaway (or Desert Islands) 108
30. Blythe Lake and Coulee 110
31. Potholes Canal 112

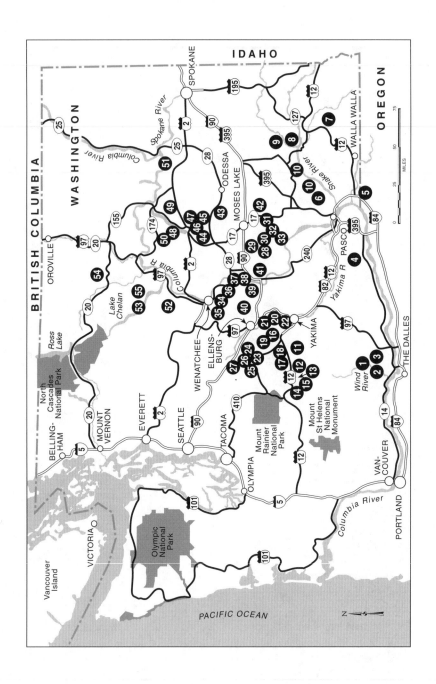

32. Crab Creek Trails 114
33. Goose Lakes Plateau 117

Wenatchee Area 119

34. Colockum Wildlife Recreation Area 120
35. Colockum Pass Road 122
36. Ancient Lakes 123
37. Dusty Lake 125
38. Frenchman Coulee 126
39. Trees of Stone 128
40. Whiskey Dick Mountain 130
41. Wanapum Breaks 131
42. East Saddle Mountain 133

Lower Grand Coulee 135

43. Summer Falls 136
44. The Grand Coulee–Lenore Lake Cave Shelters 138
45. Coulee City Stagecoach Road–Deep Lake 140
46. Monument Coulee 142
47. Dry Falls Cave 143

Upper Grand Coulee 145

48. Steamboat Rock 146
49. Northrup Canyon and Wagon Road 148
50. Giant Cave Arch 150
51. Hawk Bay 152

Northern State 155

52. Lewisia Tweedyi 156
53. Chelan Lakeshore Trail 158
54. Campbell Lake 162
55. Smith Canyon 163

Appendix: Sagebrush Country 165

Index 171

Lupine

INTRODUCTION

The Springtime Flight to Sunshine and Flowers

The Cascade Range has two sides, the one swept by the winds that blow in wetness from the ocean, the other facing the sun that dries the sky and desiccates the land and in springtime erupts more color than is dreamt of in a Wet-Sider's mossy philosophy.

The "flight" is not by the Dry-Siders. They, after all, *live* in the sunshine and flowers and know when and where to go walking to avoid the perils of fried brains. This book is primarily aimed at their cousins beyond the Cascade Crest who hear rumors of blue skies and gaudy blossoms a few miles to the east of their hometown gray drizzles and yearn to escape for a day or a weekend, to go berserk as a Viking at Lindisfarne, a Cajun at Mardis Gras, but are *afraid*. —Afraid because their knowledge of the Other Side is limited to drives over the crest to mountain trailheads in summer, when temperatures on East-Side highways often are 30 degrees higher than on Puget Sound. —Afraid because unlike the West Side, which is as poison-free as the Ireland sanitized by St. Patrick, beyond the Cascade Crest lurks the rattling Serpent. —Afraid because they have heard horror stories of swarming ORVs (off-road vehicles) and SUVs (sport utility vehicles, descendants of the WWII jeep) and ATVs (all-terrain vehicles) and 4x4s (four-wheel-drive vehicles, also known as four-wheelers and 4WDs, their "trails" designated on maps as 4WD) and dread being disgusted to death. —And finally, afraid that visitors may be treated as trespassing criminals in a landscape seemingly owned lock, stock, and barrel by ranchers, hunters, play-wheelers, the Atomic Energy Commission, the U.S. Army, and the Yakama Indian Nation.

In this book we speak to those fears, having shared them—and overcome them.

We have found that in springtime the East Side usually is no more than agreeably warm—or is agreeably cool in the dried-out downslope winds that blow briskly through the blue sky while the ocean-saturated upslope grayness is drenching the West Side—or is downright freezing at night—or night and day is snowy-arctic on the tundra-like ridges. We've learned that though the ORV and the ATV and the 4WD definitely do roam far too free for the tastes of a quiet pedestrian, the vastness of open space so dilutes their presence that the walker who takes reasonable care never need have a day ruined by wild and crazy guys riding yahoo wheels. Further, we have discovered an enormous amount of land that is fully open to the public, managed by state and federal officials who wistfully wonder why their beloved drylands have not attracted more walkers. Finally, we've come to know, respect, and in a way cherish the rattlesnake, bless the critter's timorous little heart.

Try it, West-Siders. Discover what East-Siders smugly know.

Drive east from Puget Sound City on I-90 (for example), observing as you go how the lowland drizzle intensifies to a steady rain at North Bend, then cuts off abruptly beyond Snoqualmie Pass. At Lake Keechelus the clouds are empties, at Cle Elum they thin and break, at Ellensburg the sky is blue.

A *blue* sky, as rarely is known nowadays in the West-Side smog. At night a sky of more stars than Seattle has seen since the 1930s. A *big* sky—east of the Cascades begins Montana.

Flowers. Color that starts on banks of the Columbia River in April or even late March, in following weeks flows up the slopes to the Yakima Canyon Rim, to Cleman Mountain, to Darling Mountain—three months of flowers while gardens of the High Cascades remain deep under snow.

Birds. Not concealed in forest canopies and understories but naked to the big sky, to the binoculars—and to the keen eyes of the densest population of raptors ever seen by the typical West-Sider, hunters which ride the thermals, closely following contours of the ridges in order to swoop down without warning and put the talons to a little bird or small beastie.

Big beasts. Deer. Elk. Mountain sheep. Cougars and bobcats. Coyotes, on high nights taunting their cousins who long since have joined the family circle of humankind, celebrating their own continued freedom, singing across the wildness from ridge to ridge, from Earth to Moon.

Rocks. Sedimentary and igneous and metamorphic rocks of the Cascade Mountains that divide East Side from West. The layers of basalt that flowed over parts of three states to form one of the largest lava plateaus in the world. The wrinklings of the crust that rumpled up Cascade rocks and basalt strata into ridges that thrust far eastward from the Cascades. The canyons sliced through these ridges by the Columbia and the Yakima as they kept pace with the uprising. The continental ice sheet from Canada which radically altered the landscape. The outbursts from ancient Lake Missoula, a huge body of water dammed by glaciers in western Montana, periodically busting through the ice barrier, loosing upon Eastern Washington the most gigantic floods for which geologists have found evidence, carrying as much as 20 times more water than all the world's present rivers and streams, in a few awesome days or weeks gouging the coulees of the Channeled Scablands.

Is It a Desert, or What?

The peoples who migrated from the Atlantic Seaboard westward through the forests were transfixed when they came to the shore of the "sea of grass." However, such wondrous tales were told of the New Jerusalem of the Oregon Country and, later, the golden valleys of California, that many pioneers mustered the courage to set sail in their prairie schooners, the "white tops," over the tall-grass prairies of the

Low Plains to the short-grass prairies of the High Plains and out into the sagebrush, the arid vastness the maps called "The Great American Desert."

Other pioneers, meanwhile, were moving more deliberately, step by step, from forest to tall grass to short grass. They broke the virgin sod, were rewarded by rich harvests, and accepted the myth perpetrated by town-boomers and railroaders that human settlement somehow had increased the rainfall, had pushed back the limits of desert.

But then the rains quit. The land speculators declared this was the exception to the rule; sure enough, the rains resumed, after a while. Then quit again. Each drought burned out a generation of sodbusters. The earliest refugees fled the encroaching desert this way or that, east or west, in their schooners. The next piled their families and possessions onto the Pacific railroads. The next rattled out of the Dust Bowl in *Grapes of Wrath* flivvers. The lesson of the hydrologic cycle at last struck home, that though dry and wet alternate everywhere, west of the 100th meridian there is altogether too much dry to permit sustained success with the traditional northern European methods of farming.

One definition of "desert" is an area where the annual evaporation

Lower trail to Ancient Lakes (Hike 36)

exceeds the annual precipitation. The person who lives in the 30-inch rainfall of Seattle, hikes in the 100 inches of Snoqualmie Pass, and drives east to the 9 inches of Ellensburg and the 4 or fewer inches of the Channeled Scablands, and to the 115-degree temperatures of Moses Lake in August, vehemently declares, *"That is desert!"*

Ecologists sympathize. One has commented, "If you have hot, dry summers, rattlesnakes and horned lizards, cactus and sand dunes, you tend to feel you are in a desert." Franklin and Dyrness (for this and following references, see the Appendix) acknowledge the sentiment: "The vegetation of all or portions of the rainshadow east of the Cascades is often referred to as desert, high desert, northern desert shrub, Great Basin desert, desert scrub." Taylor and Valum note use of the term "cold desert." Hitchcock and Cronquist flat-out categorize many plants as those of "desert" or "sagebrush desert."

However, neither these authorities nor any other ecologist accept the simplistic precipitation-evaporation definition of desert. Other factors enter in. For example, summers east of the Cascades certainly are hot and dry, yet the winters are cold and frosty-snowy—and long. Alpine plants of the High Cascades hurry through their sprouting, flowering, and seed-setting while the soil is briefly snow-free and the temperatures warm enough to permit life. In exactly the same manner, plants of the "cold desert" avoid the water deficit of summer by exploiting winter's frost and snow and spring's snowmelt. The East Side is not baked sterile, as is the case with true deserts, which undergo decades of unremitting year-round deficit. Things live there. Thrive there. It's as vegetatively busy as an alpine tundra.

Travelers who have been to the Sahara and the Gobi deny that there is very much desert anywhere in the United States. They grudgingly concede the status to a minor portion of Death Valley and to bits and pieces of the Mojave and the Great Salt Lake basin and various small localities from Utah and Nevada to the Southwest. However, they dispute that Edward Abbey ever in his life saw a true desert of significant size; his classic book, *Desert Solitaire,* is about something else. In any event, ecologists agree with the world travelers: there is *no desert* in Washington.

If not desert, what *is* the East Side?

Steppe, That's What

Franklin and Dyrness say, "Steppe is the more appropriate term. . . ." They distinguish three major sorts of steppe: (1) *steppe* (just plain), which might be called "grass-steppe" because it is dominated by perennial bunchgrasses and because it lacks *Artemisia tridentata* (big, or tall, sagebrush); (2) *shrub-steppe,* where the bunchgrasses share dominance with the big sagebrush; and (3) *meadow-steppe,* which occurs in Washington in the Palouse country. They count 6 million hectares of contiguous steppe, shrub-steppe, and meadow-steppe in the Columbia River Basin.

None of this book's routes lie in meadow-steppe and few in grass-steppe, which, broadly speaking, is located in southeastern Washington, and along the Columbia River upstream from Wenatchee, and in narrow fingers beside the Methow and Okanogan. Most of our routes are in shrub-steppe downstream from Wenatchee on the Columbia, on the west edge of the Columbia Plateau, and north and south of the Yakima River.

This generalization is suggestive rather than precise. Different elevations, different sun exposures, different soils and drainages produce, in the same vicinity, a variety of plant communities existing side by side. Within shrub-steppe there may be enclaves of grass-steppe, and vice versa.

Further, many of this book's routes are in a zone *between* pure sagebrush and pure forest. The rise in elevation westward towards the Cascades brings steadily more cloudiness, rain, and snow—eventually enough moisture to support vegetables much larger than sagebrush—trees. From east to west there are, first, a belt of open steppe, then of forest dominated by ponderosa pine.

The boundary is not a sharp line. Typically, in the transition zone, trees grow on valley-bottom alluvium where the water table is replenished by mountain-fed streams and/or residual snowmelt; in draws that are shadowed from the midday sun; on north slopes, which in the northern hemisphere receive fewer hours of sunshine per day than the south; on east slopes which receive the sun of morning, less hot and evaporative than the sun of afternoon; and, compounding the orientation differential, on east and north slopes because the southwesterly winds of winter storms blow snow over the ridge crests. Typically, in the transition zone, the ridge crests, south slopes, and west slopes are steppe. Another factor is that forest extends farther east where soils are coarse and stony, and nonforest farther west where soils are fine-textured.

As elevations increase westward to still more precipitation and less evaporation, the forest changes composition. Again speaking broadly, above the ponderosa pine is grand fir/Douglas fir, then white pine/whitebark pine/western larch/subalpine fir. No "desert" here, certainly? Hmmm . . . The interfingering of steppe and forest continues in some places to an interfingering with subalpine meadows; big sagebrush grows close to the glaciers on the east side of Mount Adams and to near 8000 feet on Chopaka Mountain, easternmost peak of the North Cascades.

The West-Side hiker is familiar with the *single timberline* where the forests that begin on the shores of Puget Sound yield to the subalpine meadows of the Cascades. He knits his brow when confronted by the *two* timberlines beyond the Cascade Crest. A pair of hikes described in these pages provides a textbook example. A few miles west of Yakima, Sedge Ridge lifts from the broad plain of Ahtanum Creek in beautifully naked steppe. As the crest gains elevation and thus moisture, it grows ponderosa pine and friends. Farther west, higher, wetter, and colder, the ridge culminates in Darling Mountain, where subalpine meadows intermix with groves of shrubby white and whitebark pines. This one ridge, its full length easily walked in a day, exhibits the *lower* or *dry timberline* caused by the aridity of the rainshadow and hot summers, and the *upper* or *cold timberline* caused by the frosts and snows and winds of a nine-month winter.

The plant communities below the lower timberline and above the upper share many characteristics. They are sky-open, sunbright, windswept—quite different wildlands from the deep woods. They have a very small *biomass*—a square mile of tundra or steppe may contain

Upper trail to Ancient Lakes (Hike 36)

less organic material than a single tree of the forest. Both vividly display very ancient communities which add little to the biomass but much to the color—the lichens. Both environments are so harsh that plants must make hay while the sun shines—or before it shines too much. Inches from each other are radically different microclimates, individual niches suited to highly specialized plants; the flora is enormously more diverse than that of the forest.

Many species that flourish below the dry timberline are the same or closely related to those above the cold timberline. Bewildered at seeing sagebrush beside a glacier and cactus in bloom among the bluebells, West-Siders have coined the term "desert-alpine" to describe areas that to their ignorant eyes appear to be alpine-like tundra; the scientifically more accurate name is *lithosol* (see the Appendix).

Through the Seasons in the Steppe

East-Siders are loyal to their homeland in every season and situation, and we Wet-Side carpetbaggers who fear that too much sun might endanger our immortal souls bless them and pray for them. However, we tend to feel that high summer is not the ideal season to go walking the steppe. Granted, the sun is not always so intolerably heavy a burden. When a major storm is pounding the West Side with heavy rain, ridges of the East Side typically are a circus of amusing little black-hearted squalls, exciting winds, and a scurrying of dust devils, those miniature twisters that on occasion grow big enough to take the roof off a barn or carry a tent to Oz. Whatever the weather, flowers are few or absent in summer.

Fall also lacks flowers but not color—the leaves of aspen and cottonwood backlighted to yellow torches by the lowering sun, the forests of larch (the evergreen that is not) en-goldening mountainsides, and the morning frost crystal-white on the tawny grass. However, fall is the season of another recreation and it is no use to tell hikers unaccustomed to gunfire that they simply should "wear hunter orange and not worry"; peacelovers are best advised to confine their wartime walking to, say, Sun Lakes State Park.

The hiker who wishes to see and shoot (with camera only) elk and deer should come in winter, when the animals descend from the high cold to their low refuges of yore, and there are confronted by unfriendly orchardists and retreat to the feedlots maintained by the State Wildlife Department. Winter is the season, too, for those pedestrians who attach webs or boards to their feet and wrap mufflers around their noses, but that is the subject of books other than this.

Spring, of course, is the choice season for boots-only pedestrians. In late March springtime comes to the river canyons at elevations of 2000 feet and below. In late June it reaches the ridges at 3500 feet and above. In July it moves higher to the subalpine elevations, and out of this guidebook to others. The "calendar spring" is a treacherous season, fraught with possible peril. Winter may linger on the high ridges

Elk in Tucannon Wildlife Recreation Area (Hike 7)

into April or even May; hypothermia in the sagebrush is entirely possible. Additionally, many "roads" described in these pages scarcely deserve the name, being maintained minimally or not at all. Creeks may be in snowmelt flood into April, and mud may be axle-deep until May. To identify "springtime," look not to the calendar but to the land.

How to Step the Steppe, This Book in Hand

East-Siders can step out their back doors and in minutes from the breakfast table turn rosy-red from sunburn and be half-overcome by the color and perfume of flowers, and score that for their side.

For a West-Sider, a day hike on the East Side requires so much of the re-creating day to be spent in the de-creating heck of the highway that a trip may only be justified when the craving for sunshine and flowers bursts the bounds of sanity. We carpetbagging authors often have busted the bounds in a sodden morning, fled over the crest, and returned west in evening. Our preference, however, is overnighting. Mostly we car-camp, which comparatively few folks do in spring—campgrounds that are zoos from Memorial Day to Labor Day are virtually empty earlier on. Campers able by their occupation or lack of one (retirement) to "weekend" from Monday to Friday can find solitude just about anywhere.

Fully (plushly) developed campgrounds (picnic tables, privies, garbage cans, piped water, perhaps even showers) are provided by Washington State Parks at many locations, at a few by county park departments, and here and there by private operators. A number of

National Forest campgrounds are close to steppes; their amenity level ranges from quite high to somewhat low, though sufficient for comfort.

The Washington State Department of Natural Resources (DNR) has several delightful campgrounds in the Ahtanum Multiple-Use Area; amenities are medium level. The State Wildlife Department and the U.S. Bureau of Land Management (BLM) offer a few bare-bones sites, usually not signed, only occasionally with privies, just about never with tables or trustworthy water, and usually no water at all. There are, in addition, myriad places where a car can pull off the rude track into the sagebrush and campers can roll out the sleeping bags. A 5-gallon water-carrier, filled at home, is a reservoir sufficient for a single overnight of two adults, one child, and two medium-size dogs; refills with trustworthy water are easily obtained at gas stations. An ice chest keeps the milk and lettuce and root beer cool. A camp stove heats

Northrup Lake (Hike 49)

the beans and weenies and fries the bacon and eggs—at many campsites there is next to no wood (and nowadays, mighty few buffalo chips). Folding chairs and tables are optional. Few backpackers have gotten onto what great things await them on the steppe. The Chelan Lakeshore Trail (partly steppe) has become known across the nation as an American classic. The Yakima Rim Skyline Trail (all steppe) is yet to receive its equally merited fame. These two routes are, however, the merest introduction. To be sure, formally designated trails are few, most routes follow old wagon or jeep tracks or simply strike off through the sagebrush and scabrock, and there are very few established camps, but the walk-anywhere country of the steppe is equally camp-anywhere country.

Steppe backpacking is in most respects identical to tundra backpacking; a special manual is not needed, though a beginner may wish to consult *Backpacking: One Steppe at a Time* or any other of the genre. The central differences are: (1) Don't plan on a wood fire—cook on a stove or eat cold, pull on your sweater or crawl in your bag; (2) Stay out of your tent unless absolutely forced to retreat from frost or wind—there are no stars to be seen in a tent and the songs of the coyote are muted; (3) Assume that your route will have no safe water and carry your own supply—a gallon a day per person. The reward? Though the steppe has grievously too little designated national, state, or local wilderness, it nevertheless has, de facto if not de jure, a vast expanse of wildness. A person can be more lonesome on the steppe than in the average national park or national wilderness, see at least as many flowers (though not trees), and surely hear more coyotes.

Most of our routes are indeterminate in objective and thus length and elevation gain lend themselves to a number of variations. Users of our other hiking guides will note differences in the presentation of data here. We have named the applicable USGS map but usually have not listed other useful maps. The state parks often have informative leaflets. Map shops and bookstores sell road maps and portfolios of USGS-derived maps that are just about indispensable for poking about on tracks pioneered by wagons, followed by war-surplus jeeps, and now, happily, increasingly banned to public wheels for the sake of preserving native plants and wildlife habitat.

Of Snakes and Ticks and Seeds in Your Breathable Shoes

The equipment for steppe-walking is about the same as for walking anywhere. Footwear, however, demands a word or two. First, sturdy boots generally are mandatory; the rock-blocky footing of lava land is too rough for the light shoes that serve very well on forest paths. Second, the steppe is so seedy that a hiker in breathable-fabric "hot-weather" boots may come home with feet looking like victims of the porky pine, sharp little seeds having slid through the fabric and socks to punch holes in the skin; wear impenetrable leather or rubber boots.

Summer Falls, as it used to be (Hike 43)

We have not felt compelled to dwell, here, on giardiasis, because *Giardia* inhabit West-Side waters as well as East-Side, wilderness and city alike. This is not to minimize the unpleasantness of the exercise that used to be known as the "Boy Scout trots" and surely not the life-threatening danger of hepatitis. We suggest that every backpacker, East-Side, West-Side, upside-and-down, study the discussion in *Medicine for Mountaineering,* by Dr. James A. Wilkerson. He warns that jet-trekkers inevitably will be bringing home from Asia and Africa bugs more lethal than American wildlands yet have seen. Learn to boil. Treat with iodine (not chlorine). Be wary of over-advertised patent filters.

Neither will we linger here on the other loathsome and dangerous maladies transmitted by ticks. For one thing, ticks are on the West Side as well as the East. For another, medicine is the business of Dr. Jim's book, not ours. Ditto about poison oak—it's on both sides of the Cascades; we have seen a lot more on beaches of south Puget Sound than on the East Side.

Now, to the main event . . .

There are folks who've lived their whole lives on the East Side and never seen a rattlesnake. Most have done so, of course, often enough to get used to serpents and be amused by West-Siders who leap high in the sky at the "rattling" of flying crickets. Still, just as a resident of Puget Sound City learns, very early on, to look both ways before crossing the street, east of the Cascade Crest he must learn to look all ways for rattlers—which are far less dangerous than vehicles on streets (or trails). The basic facts are these:

Most snakes are not rattlers. (But the West-Sider is unlikely to be able to make a quick identification and may wish to look upon all reptiles as threats, and that's not entirely stupid.)

Even gigantic snakes are timid. If they hear you coming, they'll often skedaddle. If they can't (as when trapped), they'll rattle (unless they're wet or shedding and unable to do so); if the hiker is as deaf as one of this book's authors, the rattling is not sufficient warning.

Little snakes may be more dangerous than big snakes. The latter are older and have learned not to strike except to prepare a meal for eating or to defend against attack. The former are younger, inexperienced, and haven't figured out the rules of the road.

Even when coiled, a snake can strike only about one-third of its body length—at the maximum, 1 or 2 feet.

Snakes are *ectotherms,* unable to shiver or sweat, relying on the environment for warming and cooling. In winter they must hibernate; in the Washington steppe they generally are holed up from November or so until early April or so. Snakeophobes can walk the sagebrush during that time free of fear. Sadly, in that period there are sun and sky and rocks and perhaps big animals and possibly cross-country skiing, but no flowers. As the flowers come out, so do the snakes. You can't have the blossoms without the rattles.

The following rules of travel are helpful.

Unable as they are to regulate body temperature by internal mechanisms, snakes must somehow cool off in the heat, warm up in the cold.

Rattlesnake

After chilly nights, watch for them atop sunny rocks. In the midday sun, be suspicious of little caves in cliffs and rockslides; before crawling over a log to the shady side, take a look. Be particularly cautious at springs and beside streams; snakes cannot live without water and in baked terrain spend most of their time handy to wetness, which is also coolness; they are common in riparian meadows and shrub—in the thick brush and the lush grass, alas.

Walk watchfully. An inspection several feet ahead suffices; this becomes as automatic as watching for cars on city streets. We describe several walks along (little-traveled) roads, where snakes are so highly visible the most nervous West-Sider can feel easy; these routes are especially good for Irishmen and other beginners.

Walk noisily, singing and chattering and banging a rattlesnake stick or ice ax on rocks. Give notice of your coming.

Avoid brushy draws where a walker must crash blindly through greenery. Do not clamber up a cliff or cutbank without ascertaining what's up there where your face is about to be.

In grass, sweep the snake stick around; if one is in there it likely will attack the stick.

Leave your shorts and skintight jeans on the West Side. Hike the East Side in baggy pants of tough cloth. In the springtime you won't sweat too much.

If you hike with a dog, keep it on leash or make it heel.

—And so, you get bit by a snake. What then? First off, sit down, relax, breathe deeply, be calm, wait for treatment or evacuation by a qualified rescue team (summoned by sending Lassie to fetch the nearest county sheriff). Hold the happy thoughts that: it may not have been a rattler or may merely have gummed you; more Americans die of bee stings than snakebites; most snakebite deaths in the United States are in the Southeast, among children crawling about their backyards and cultists proving their faith.

Second, if a companion comes at you brandishing a snakebite kit and proposes to whack your veins with a razor blade and inject you with antivenin, ward him off with your rattlesnake stick while he produces his Red Cross certificate or other credentials. It is a well-established medical fact that in the hands of an untrained person a snakebite kit is more dangerous than a snake. Wait for the arrival of an expert, or until you feel well enough to walk out unaided. Meanwhile, watch out for bees.

Managers, and Management, of the Steppe

Except for several cases specified in the text, all the walks in this book are on public land. The managers may, or may not, be able to provide the walker necessary or useful information, depending on the funding and thus the staffing of the various agencies involved.

The most extensive management is that of the Washington State Department of Wildlife (formerly, Game), with 743,000 acres east of the Cascades, organized in Wildlife Recreation Areas (WRA; formerly, Game Ranges). As an example of the amounts of land involved, just one of the areas, the L. T. Murray WRA, has 103,000 acres—160 square miles. Much of the department's holdings were acquired with funds obtained from the selling of hunting licenses. The steady decline in the numbers of hunters has progressively impoverished the agency, and though general state appropriations for recreation have been available from time to time, they have not been enough to hold the line. As the department's responsibilities have been expanded to include non-game wildlife, and as nonconsumptive recreation has enormously increased, no means has been found to channel, for example, hikers' fees to hiking trails.

The lack of money originally dictated the department's philosophy of minimum facilities, minimum maintenance. Just because a road is shown on the map, the visitor should never assume it will be passable. However, more influential nowadays than poverty is mission—WRA roads (wheel tracks, that is) are being closed to public vehicles to preserve the wildlife habitat. The serendipity for the wildland walker is that the human population density is kept low, and thus the noise level. It even is possible, increasingly so, to find refuges from wheels, places where a backpacker or horse camper could set up a backcountry domicile certain there will be no middle-of-the-night visitation by an SUV horde of teenage keggers or drunken "hunters."

A second principal manager of the steppe is Washington State Parks. Most of its establishments feature almost urban-like campgrounds, jammed full in summer but generally ample for all comers in spring, except on Memorial Day. The text herein describes the parks that offer inviting trail systems—trails designed for nonconsumptive recreation, thus attractive in hunting season, and typically motor-free or even foot-only.

The Washington State Department of Natural Resources is represented in this book solely by the Ahtanum Multiple-Use Area, which cannot be accepted as the model for the future. Granted, the local folks have much need for space to exercise their 4WDs, ATVs, ORVs, snowmobiles, and dirtbikes. However, the "multiple-use" here omits quiet travel on foot or horse. It is our opinion such provision could be made without seriously diminishing the machine-running opportunities. The local management has done a commendable job on campgrounds, which are delightful bases for hiking during that "window" between snowmobile season and ORV season. Exploiting tricks of the terrain and conditions of the snow, we have been clever enough to find routes that even now are much worth walking, even backpacking. If you feel (as we do) that these are insufficient, don't harass the busy people in charge of the local office. Write the boss: The Honorable Jennifer Belcher, State Land Commissioner, Olympia, WA 98504.

The National Wildlife Service has jurisdiction over several National Wildlife Refuges treated herein; adequate information for hiking is available on-site during a visit.

The U.S. Bureau of Land Management (BLM) maintains three recreation sites (Roza, Umtanum, and Squaw Creek) in the Yakima River Canyon; no advance information necessary; just pull the car off the highway and walk or picnic or fish or camp or what you will, subject only to comment by neighbors or the State Highway Patrol. For the hiker, the one significant responsibility of the BLM hereabouts is the Juniper Dunes Wilderness, which the agency opposed but whose establishment by Congress it has accepted. Write: U.S. Department of the Interior, Bureau of Land Management, 1133 North Western Avenue, Wenatchee, WA 98801.

The U.S. Forest Service oversees Conrad Meadows, part of Lake Chelan, and bits of other routes herein; the National Park Service, part of Lake Chelan. Telephone the agencies' joint information service in Seattle.

Further information about these lands can be obtained using the addresses listed in the Appendix.

In this book we have avoided privately owned ranchlands. A person driving around the East Side will spot innumerable foot-beckoning routes, many readily accessible from interstate highway rest areas or state highway turnouts. Many can be walked by visitors without objection by the owners. In our opinion it would be reasonable for a state agency to enter into agreement with ranchers to open certain of their lands to public foot-and-horse recreation; in some cases this already has been done.

We have avoided lands of the Yakama Indian Nation out of respect for their wishes and many millennia of residence and for the shameful history of a century of invasions of their ancestral lands. We hope someday to see carefully regulated (by the Yakama Nation) public recreation made a source of fee income for these property owners.

We have stayed out of the third of a million (or so) acres of the Yakima Firing Center. Let it be noted to the Army's credit that maneuvers are scheduled to avoid disturbing wildlife during seasons crucial to perpetuating the species. (War sometimes can be less cruel to the land than peacetime busy-ness and frolicking; contrast the prairies in Fort Lewis with the adjoining sprawl of Puget Sound City.)

Finally, we have shunned the Hanford Atomic Energy Reservation. However, no complaints. The fencing of the reservation has excluded 4WDs and ATVs and guns since 1944; grazing by sheep and cows ceased in 1967. Fully a fifth of the reservation is in an Arid Lands Ecology Reserve designated by the Department of Ecology as an Ecology Research Park. *This is the largest expanse of pristine (or near-pristine) steppe in the Northwest* and the only area in the United States that has been set aside exclusively for the study of shrub-steppe ecology. We are content not to have our boots intruding.

A Note About Safety

Safety is an important concern in all outdoor activities. No guidebook can alert you to every hazard or anticipate the limitations of every reader. Therefore, the descriptions of roads, trails, routes, and natural features in this book are not representations that a particular place or excursion will be safe for your party. When you follow any of the routes described in this book, you assume responsibility for your own safety. Under normal conditions, such excursions require the usual attention to traffic, road and trail conditions, weather, terrain, the capabilities of your party, and other factors. Keeping informed on current conditions and exercising common sense are the keys to a safe, enjoyable outing.

Right: *Burrowing owl.*
Below: *Mule deer.*

Opposite, clockwise from top left:
Yellow bell; iris; stonecrop; bitter cherry. Right: *Mountain bluebird.* Below: *Small mertensia.*

Opposite top: *Redwing blackbird's nest.* Opposite bottom: *Keeping a watchful eye.* Above: *Same nest 15 days later.*

Top left: *Grass widow.*
Top right: *Grosbeak.*
Bottom: *Bitterroot*
(Lewisia rediviva).
Opposite: *Shooting star.*

Opposite: *Sand tracks at Two Sisters Rocks (Hike 5).* Right: *Grasshopper.* Below: *Rattlesnake.*

Top: *Bighorn sheep, Tucannon Wildlife Recreation Area (Hike 7).*
Bottom: *Redwing blackbird.*

SOUTHERN STATE

Two Sisters Rocks (Hike 5)

LYLE-TO-GOLDENDALE RAILS-TO-TRAILS: SWALE CANYON

Length: one way 13 miles
High point: 1150 feet
Elevation gain: 1070 feet
Management: Washington State Parks
USGS map: Staker Butte

The Lyle-to-Goldendale Rails-to-Trail conversion will provide 31 miles of horse/hiker trail and bikeway. The first 18 miles in the Klickitat River Canyon are within sight of Highway 142; short river-bank walks appear very attractive. However, for hikers the central attraction is the 13 roadless miles of Swale Canyon from Wahkicus on the Klickitat River upstream to Warwick on the edge of farmland. Another 13 miles through farmland to Goldendale will not be maintained. At this writing, planning is still in progress and reconstruction has not yet begun. The February 1996 flood removed big chunks of the road-bed, making some sections impassable.

The state park's right-of-way through the V-shaped Swale Canyon is only a few feet wide, no room for camping. The springtime green is heavily dotted with flowers but no trees. For shade bring a beach umbrella.

Drive the Columbia River Highway to the hamlet of Lyle some 75 miles east of Vancouver.

For short walks along the Klickitat River and in lower Swale Canyon, go north from Lyle on Lyle-Klickitat-Goldendale road No. 142 upstream along the Klickitat River some 18 miles to unsigned Wahkicus

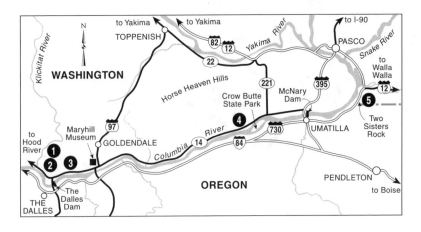

and park near the rail bridge opposite Swale Canyon. The ties on the bridge have not yet been covered, so cross with care.

For the Warwick start, from the east side of Lyle drive the Lyle-Centerville-Goldendale road (unsigned in 1996) to a crossing of Swale Creek and the rails-to-trail at the top of the canyon. For parking drive on a bit farther to Warwick. The first mile down to the canyon is in farm country; the rock walls then rise higher and the canyon grows lonesomer.

There are "Closed—No Trespassing" notices posted, but according to the State Parks people, this publically owned right-of-way is definitely open to nonmotorized use from Lyle 31 miles to Warwick. Hopefully, the route will become a National Recreation Trail and be gracefully accepted by locals. For more information or concerns about access, call the State Parks office.

Rails-to-Trails along the Klickitat River

2 CHERRY ORCHARD TRAIL

Length: round trip 1/4 to 4 miles
High point: 1000 feet
Elevation gain: 900 feet
Management: Cherry Orchard Preserve
USGS maps: Lyle, The Dalles North

The traveler driving east up the Columbia Gorge here comes upon the first Central Washington steppe open to his/her boots. The views and meadows are worth every bit of sweat. But look sharp! There are lots of ticks in April and May, and always poison ivy, poison oak, and snakes. The hiking is thanks to the gracious permission by the owner of the Cherry Orchard Preserve so mind your manners.

Drive Columbia River Highway 14 east about 2.5 miles from the

Columbia River and volcanic outcrop

hamlet of Lyle, through two tunnels, and between mileposts 77 and 78 find a large (unsigned) trailhead parking spot on the left side of the highway.

The trail climbs steeply through an oak forest. In a few feet cross a fence on a stile and continue up to an abandoned road. Go left a short bit to a Cherry Orchard Trail sign. Sign in.

For the sampling, stay on the old road to a striking viewpoint, directly above the parking lot, of the river and basalt flows piled one atop the other. For the big show continue up through the oaks to grassland dotted by flowers and clumps of poison oak. At ³/₄ mile either wander off to sniff the meadow perfumes or continue to the ridge top for bigger and bigger views.

Beginning of the Cherry Orchard Trail

3 HORSETHIEF LAKE STATE PARK

USGS map: Staker Butte

In an area of outstanding attractions, three features make Horsethief Lake State Park extra-special: a famous pictograph to ponder, a rugged butte to climb, and an abandoned farm to explore.

She-Who-Watches

Length: round trip ²/₃ mile
High point: 250 feet (approximate)
Elevation gain: 70 feet (approximate)

What does she watch from her viewpoint high in the lava cliffs above the Columbia River? In 1805 she would have seen Lewis and Clark pause, on their way to the ocean, to observe hundreds of Indians spearing and netting salmon as they had done for many centuries.

As with most pictographs (paintings on the rock surface) and petroglyphs (carvings in the rock surface), the meaning is a mystery.

She-Who-Watches, an Indian pictograph

One explanation is that when a man returning from a journey wished to know if his woman had been faithful during his absence, he'd walk her by the eyes. If She-Who-Watches frowned, bad news.

On the Washington side of the Columbia, opposite the Oregon city of The Dalles, drive SR 14 to Horsethief Lake State Park and the parking area nearest the river, elevation 180 feet.

A well-defined trail heads west from the parking lot through a field. Just short of a swamp it turns right, ascends a rocky slope, threads up and down among basalt outcrops, ducks under a barbed-wire fence, passes several pictographs, and ends under She-Who-Watches. However, the threat of vandalism in this era of hoodlums with spray cans has forced the fencing-off of the pictographs. In summer park rangers lead visitors or groups. Call (509) 767-1159 for information and reservations.

Horsethief Butte

Length: round trip ½ to 1½ miles
High point: 500 feet (approximate)
Elevation gain: 200 feet (approximate)

The lava blocks and towers, the deep creases and clefts, the walls and benches of Horsethief Butte provide a wealth of wildflowers and topographical surprises. Views are broad over the boat-dotted waters of the Columbia River and Horsethief Lake (Reservoir) and to the snows of Mount Hood. In the springtime climbers throng to practice their rock technique.

Drive SR 14 east 1.3 miles from the Horsethief Lake State Park entrance to a two-car parking spot on the north side of the highway, elevation 288 feet.

From the south side of the highway a well-defined trail approaches the base of the butte, appearing certain to dead-end at the near-vertical north wall. Surprise! The steepening path finds a break in the precipice and climbs 200 feet to the summit. That is, almost. The 498-foot summit actually is plural, split by gullies into several tops. Scrambling is possible to any of the lot for the panorama of sun-baked basalt, wind-rippled water, and gleaming glaciers.

But the exploration has only begun. An easy path down the southwest side of the summit area leads to the next surprise, a wide shelf between cliffs above and cliffs below. Walk the shelf south to an overlook of river and railroad.

For another surprise—a circle route all the way around the butte—follow the bench eastward until it peters out. A very faint, narrow trail follows the contours of the steep hillside, safe enough for the surefooted, though the cliffs above and below could unsettle the horizons of a person subject to vertigo. In the middle of the steepness an abandoned barbed-wire fence must be stepped over. Thereafter the slope eases and the rest of the circuit is easy.

Dalles Mountain Ranch

Length: round trip ½ to 6 miles
High point: 3220 feet
Elevation gain: 2000 feet

A former 6123-acre cattle ranch stretching over 4 square miles is free for the roaming. Most of the spread is too steep and rocky to grow grain, but the grass fed cattle for over a century. The house and a small barn have been repaired and remodeled so many times it's hard to tell what parts are really old.

Dalles Mountain Ranch State Park adjoins the 3000-acre Columbia Hills Natural Area Preserve managed by the Department of Natural

Dalles Mountain Ranch

Resources. The park ranger told us that to protect three rare plant species and examples of native plants, the preserve is closed to the public, but an official handout said the hard-surface road through the preserve can be walked to a communication tower on the crest of the Columbia Hills. Better check first.

Drive Columbia River Highway 14 just 0.9 mile east of the Highway 197 junction (to Dalles, Oregon) and go left on the Dalles Mountain Road (gravel) 3.5 miles to the ranch marked with an old farm wagon. A few feet farther, on the left, is a parking area near an iron shed.

Walk back to the wagon and up the road towards the modern farmhouse. Follow the road as far as you want or take off over the open meadows to Eightmile Stream.

4 CROW BUTTE

Length: round trip 1½ to 2½ miles
High point: 671 feet
Elevation gain: 370 feet
Management: Crow Butte State Park, Umatilla National Wildlife Refuge
USGS maps: Crow Butte, Blalock Island, Paterson

The John Day Dam drowned 76 miles of the Columbia River. As partial mitigation for the ecological disaster, in 1969 some 18 miles of "lake" (Lake Wallula) were put in the Umatilla National Wildlife Refuge. Much of the preserve is managed to grow corn, sunflowers, wheat, alfalfa, and wheatgrass for waterfowl. Other lands are left for nature to manage, supplying native foods and cover for birds and animals.

Crow Butte is an excellent spot to sample the vicinity of the refuge. Its domed summit provides broad views of the "lake," the largest reservoir in the Columbia Gorge. At the base of the butte are unexpected serendipities in a land of sagebrush: sand dunes for sliding and a sandy beach for swimming.

Drive SR 14 east from Maryhill or west 14 miles from Paterson to Crow Butte State Park, named not for the bird but Mr. Crow, who homesteaded hereabouts in the 1850s. Park in the day-use area, elevation 300 feet.

Walk through the motor-home parking lot and between campsites No. 40 and 42 find the trailhead signed "Crow Summit 0.8 miles and Sandy Beach 0.8 miles." Ascend the obvious wheel track (closed to vehicles). In a scant 1/2 mile keep right, sidehilling upward. When the grade levels, climb to the grassy ridge and follow deer tracks

Sand dunes at the foot of Crow Butte

Great horned owl

along the crest to the rocky summit, 671 feet, about ³/₄ mile from the campground.

For the full picture in all directions, climb both summits. The most exciting view is downstream, over the riverside dunes and beach to Mount Hood. Return to the wheel track and contour southward to a junction. Go left, down to the dunes and a delightful beach, also about ³/₄ mile from the camp.

5 TWO SISTERS (TWO CAPTAINS) ROCKS

Length: round trip ¹/₂ to 1 mile
High point: 500 feet (approximate)
Elevation gain: 200 feet (approximate)
Management: Walla Walla County

A pair of uncannily statue-like basalt towers stands guard over Wallula Gap, where the Columbia River cuts through the Horse Heaven Hills. Walla Walla County, guardian of the landmark, has erected a readerboard that tells of three sisters who married Old Coyote. He loved his wives so dearly that he turned two into rocks and the third into a nearby cave. Unaware of the legend, Albert Salisbury, who chronicled the expedition of Captains Lewis and Clark, thought the rocks a fitting tribute to them. Take your pick. Or, why not take both?

Drive US 730 between Umatilla and Kennewick. Coming from the west, at milepost 4 in Washington spot a small parking area on the south side of the highway. Coming from the east, find the parking area at 1.9 miles from the intersection of US 12 and US 730. Elevation, 380 feet.

A stile is provided to cross over the barbed-wire fence; if that seems too tricky, crawl under. Ascend steeply ¼ mile to a prairie flat and a split in the trail. One fork climbs very steeply to the base of the rocks. The other circles them to a group of small sand dunes and wanders across little prairies to viewpoints over the river.

Two Sisters Rocks and the Columbia River

$\overline{\underline{6}}$ JUNIPER DUNES WILDERNESS

Length: round trip from north trailhead 1 to 3 miles; from south trailhead 12 miles
High point: 900 feet (approximate)
Elevation gain: 70 feet (approximate)
Management: U.S. Bureau of Land Management
USGS map: Levey NE

Sand patterns, Juniper Dunes Wilderness

The area used to be called (rather tongue-in-cheek) "Juniper Forest," to recognize the most northerly (nearly) reach of the western juniper. When Congress, in 1984, placed 7000 acres under the protective umbrella of the Wilderness Act, it focused instead on the state of Washington's closest approach to genuine desert—huge sand dunes ever on the march, other dunes partly anchored by sparse vegetation, and little groves of shrubby trees. Hundreds of square miles surrounding the preserve grow wheat. Here is an oasis of wildland sand.

Drive US 12 east from Pasco towards Walla Walla to 2 miles past the interchange of US 12 and US 395. At 1.5 miles short of the

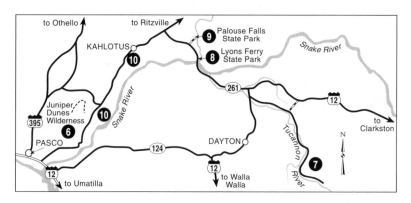

Juniper Dunes Wilderness

Snake River bridge, turn east on Kahlotus Road—and make a choice between two trailheads.

For the "official" trailhead on the south side of the Wilderness, drive Kahlotus Road 5.7 miles to a crop-spraying facility and turn left on Peterson Road (gravel; sign missing in 1996) 4.5 miles to an obscure parking lot, elevation 830 feet. "Official" though this trailhead may be, the route is roughly 6 miles to the dunes the visitor has come to see. A long walk. Camping is allowed; no fires, of course; no water except in your canteens.

The north trailhead exists through the philanthropy of a farmer. The dunes are little more than a stone's throw from the road. However, to protect the benefactor's crops, the trailhead is closed from June 15 to September 15. Even when open, there is no overnight parking and thus no camping.

To reach the north trailhead, continue on Kahlotus Road for 24 miles from US 12. Just short of a schoolhouse go left on Snake River Road. After 3.5 twisty miles, leave pavement and go left on the gravel East Blackman Ridge Road 2.4 miles, then left on Joy Road. In a final 2 miles pass Juniper Dunes Ranch to the road-end, elevation 830 feet. Do not block the benefactor's access to his fields.

Cross private land on a well-defined trail, taking care to close stock gates that you may open to get by. The way enters the Wilderness and climbs a sandy path to the top of the first dune. Go from here, where and how you please, on a network of paths to dunes and "forests," to grasses and flowers and birds, to miles of roaming in "Washington's Sahara."

Warning: One sand dune looks a whole lot like another. Keep track of where you are and where you came from. The lost rover is sure to emerge from the Wilderness eventually, but more than likely in a wheat field a dozen or so miles from the car. Don't put too much trust in the USGS map; the dunes have shifted since the map was drawn in 1964.

Until 1984 the dunes were marauded by motorcycles, dune buggies, ATVs, and ORVs. These vehicles have now been excluded but their tracks will be evident in this fragile landscape well into the next century.

7 TUCANNON RIVER

Length: round trip 3 to 8 miles
High point: 3000 feet (approximate)
Elevation gain: 800 to 2500 feet (approximate)
Management: Tucannon Wildlife Recreation Area
USGS maps: Hopkins Ridge, Panjab Creek

Valley bottoms and north slopes of the Blue Mountains foothills typically are forested, while ridge crests and south slopes generally are open steppe, flower-rich in spring, tromped in winter by hundreds of

Elk on Abeis Ridge, Tucannon Wildlife Recreation Area

elk and deer and a small band of bighorn sheep. Wherever the flowers are in bloom the animals have already moved on and up, following the receding snowline; the walker who seeks both wildlife and wildflowers must come in March for animals and again in May for flowers.

From US 12 between Dayton and Pomeroy, drive south on Tucannon River Road, signed "Camp Wooten E.L.C. 30 miles" (actually, it's only 28). Just short of 21 miles, near a cement bridge, Forest Service road No. (4700)020 goes left along Cummings Creek, elevation 2100 feet.

This is the first "trailhead"; in spring (and maybe all year) the road is gated against wheels. Walk about 1¼ miles to the second spur road on the left. Ascend this steep track to endless meadows on Abels Ridge and a remarkable view up the valley of Cummings Creek.

For the second "trailhead" continue on Tucannon River Road and turn left toward W. T. Wooten Environmental Center. Cross the river

Tucannon River valley

and go right, pass the campground to the Hixon Canyon road No. (4700)150—gated against wheels, elevation 2700 feet. Walk it 800 feet and climb open slopes to the left.

The third choice is the highest, with the smallest meadows and the steepest walking. Continue 1.3 miles on Tucannon River Road and go right on road No. (4700)180 (unmarked in 1996) 600 feet to the road-end in a gravel pit, elevation 2800 feet. Walk it 500 feet and climb the ridge to the right. From the top look up the Tucannon valley and down the Tucannon valley.

8 CHIEF OLD BONES

Length: round trip 1 to 2 miles
High point: 950 feet
Elevation gain: 150 to 400 feet
Management: Lyons Ferry State Park
USGS map: Starbuck West

When Chief Old Bones was a boy, the Great Migration on the Oregon Trail hadn't yet happened, nor had the Whitmans been massacred, and folks in his village were still talking about the Lewis and Clark Expedition. When he died in 1916, aged 89, his old bones were buried high on a lava rampart above the confluence of the Palouse and the Snake; that confluence is now drowned by Lower Monumental Dam. Upon construction of the dam, the chief was joined by occupants of a graveyard who were moved here when their ancient homes were inundated. Gaze over the tawny prairies and the tamed waters. Reflect on a dozen millennia of human history. Then explore.

Gravestone

Drive SR 261 to the north side of the Snake River crossing and the day-use area of Lyons Ferry State Park, elevation 560 feet. The trail starts at the north end. (The first 1/4 mile can be bypassed by driving the ranger's residence road to an upper parking lot.)

In 3/4 mile the broad graveled trail climbs some 400 feet above the reservoir waters to the open

Snake River

shelter, visible from below, and the grave at 950 feet. The views from the overlook are big. For even better views continue to cliffs above the Palouse Canyon. For the very best, proceed northward up another ¼ mile to the crest of the hogback ridge or return down the trail a bit and walk the splintery crest of the ridge running south.

9   PALOUSE FALLS

Length: round trip to top of falls 1 mile; bench walk 2 miles
High point: 970 feet
Elevation gain: on return 300 feet (approximate)
Management: Lyons Ferry State Park
USGS map: Palouse Falls

It's a jaded tourist, indeed, who drives past Palouse Falls without stopping to gape and gasp. And it's surely a most incurious hiker who doesn't speculate on explorations of black walls of layered lava, the flowery steppe benches between the flows, and the river flowing at the bottom of the canyon. The experienced, surefooted pedestrian can traverse those benches or teeter on the lip of the falls—but only if willing and able to negotiate paths that are steep, skiddy, and totally unmaintained.

Drive SR 261 from Washtucna 15 miles towards the Snake River and turn left on the gravel road to Palouse Falls State Park. Elevation, 970 feet.

Because of the danger of falling rock, the trail to the foot of the falls has been closed. There is, however, an undeveloped route to the top of the falls. Walk north from the parking area along the gorge rim to a short but potentially dangerous descent to the railroad, then follow a wide trail down to the river and a traverse at water's edge to the falls.

Do not be inveigled by apparent shortcuts through the cliffs from bench to bench. These paths were made by people looking for an easy way down—but there isn't any.

Palouse Falls

For the bench walk (solitude just about guaranteed) follow the canyon rim south from the parking lot to a super-steep but relatively easy 30-foot drop onto the tracks of the Union Pacific Railroad, whose Portland–Spokane branch goes through the park so entrenched in tunnels and cuts (with only occasional views) that a person hardly knows it is there. Walk the tracks some 600 feet south to a steep and, for a bit, slippery path—this is definitely not a trail for children or the timid. Before starting down, take a good look (and if you're going to, this is the best place to turn back). The trail descends steeply to a wide, grassy bench between cliffs that form a 100-foot-high wall above, and, below, a frightening 200-foot drop to the river. Very briefly this bench shrinks to a width of 12 inches but most of the way it's wide and simple for 1/2 mile to a broad prairie stomped up by deer. When the bench peters out, turn back.

10 PASCO–FISH LAKE–SPOKANE RAILS-TO-TRAILS

Management: Central Ferry State Park
USGS maps: Kahlotus, Lower Monumental Dam, Benge, Laymont, Cheney, Amber

The 130 miles of the route start at the Snake River, climb Devils Canyon to Kahlotus, cross intermixed farmland and basalt cliffs past Washtuca, cross the long trestle over Cow Creek, traverse coulees, lakes, scabland, a corner of Turnbull National Wildlife Refuge, and end in Cheney—the entire way open as of 1996 to nonmotorized travel *only*. Though few hikers (unlike bicyclists and equestrians) will care to undertake the full distance, numerous road-crossings allow many walks of 1 to 4 round-trip hours to rewarding destinations.

Be warned: the route is still covered with coarse, sharp railroad ballast. Mean on the feet.

State Parks expects to have 50 to 60 miles surfaced for walking by the year 2000 or so. The rest will be tidied up as funds are available.

Snake River Off-Road Walk

Length: round trip sampler 2 to 4 miles; to Burr Canyon 20 miles
USGS map: Lower Monumental Dam

The many miles of roadless banks along the Snake River in Washington have few public accesses and no foot trails. The 10 miles of rails-to-trails conversion between Snake River Junction and Burr Canyon are thus the more welcome.

To drive to the Snake River Junction end, from US 12 on the north

Devils Canyon tunnel near Kahlotus

side of the Snake River bridge go east on Pasco–Kahlotus Road 24 miles, turn right on Snake River Road another 5.2 miles, and park at the station site, about 60 feet above the water.

Head upriver across a large fill and under some cliffs. (Actually, in this stretch an abandoned river-level railroad grade, now a 4WD track, is easier to walk than the trail.) At the Burr Canyon end the rail-trail has climbed 360 feet above the river and is inaccessible from Burr Road, so a one-way trip is not recommended. However, the parallel railroad bed at river level can be accessed at Burr Canyon.

To drive to the Burr Canyon end, take Pasco–Kahlotus Road to 0.5 mile short of Kahlotus, go south on Lower Monumental Dam Road to Windust Park, and continue 2.2 miles to a parking spot where the river-level railroad grade crosses the road. Walk south on the rail-trail a short ¹/₂ mile where a missing culvert stops the 4WDs and gives hikers trouble too.

Devils Canyon

Length: round trip 3 miles

A spectacular canyon sliced through basalt cliffs interspersed with rockslides and green slopes. The thrill is a ³⁄₄-mile tunnel. Though from one portal you can see daylight out the other, it gets awful dark in there. Do not enter without a flashlight.

Drive Pasco–Kahlotus Road (see above). Between Kahlotus and Lower Monumental Dam Road choose a wide spot to park. Walk a short spur road and descend the few feet to the rail-trail. Walk past the gate and through the tunnel into the wild and remote-feeling Devils Canyon. Lower Monumental Dam Road also descends the canyon but is far above, out of sight except for a guardrail.

Benge

Length: round trip 2 to 10 miles

Pothole lakes and bare rocks testify to the gigantic floods that funneled through the Columbia Basin some 20,000 years ago, when the ice dam in Montana broke (repeatedly) and the enormous glacial lake emptied (repeatedly) in a matter of a few days.

Basalt outcrops along the trail near Benge

Drive Washtucan–Benge Road to the attractive village of Benge and access to the rail-trail.

In the southern direction, the rail-trail parallels the road several miles, then crosses Cow Creek on a long trestle. A few miles in the other direction the rail-trail is crossed by Benge–Winona Road in the area of rocky outcroppings.

Folsom Lake

Length: round trip 3 miles

Drive road No. 23, between Sprague and St. John, to the village of Lamont and turn right on Hardy Road. Park near the rail-trail and walk northward to the lake and beyond.

Turnbull National Wildlife Refuge

Length: round trip 6 to 10 miles

The forest might seem to disqualify this stretch for a sagebrush book. However, the lakes and wildlife are too good to pass up. From Cheney drive south 1.4 miles on Cheney–Plaza Road, park on the shoulder near the railroad overpass, and walk southwest past Long Lake.

Trail on the edge of Turnbull National Wildlife Refuge

YAKIMA AREA

Elk-trampled St. Helens ash at edge of Conrad Meadows (Hike 15)

‖ SEDGE RIDGE

Length: round trip 8 miles
High point: 4800 feet
Elevation gain: 500 feet, on return 800 feet
Management: Washington Department of Natural Resources
USGS maps: Tampico, Pine Mtn., Foundation Ridge, Piscoe Meadow
DNR map: Ahtanum Multiple-Use Area

Sedge Ridge thrusts a great, long tundra-steppe highland out east between the forks of Ahtanum Creek, pointing straight at Yakima. In the other direction it rises to pine forest, then subalpine forest, and at last to meadows and glaciers of the Goat Rocks. The ridge is a sublime connector between sagebrush country and icefield country; the walker learns with John Muir that "everything in the universe is hitched to everything else." More good news: though located in the Ahtanum Multiple-Use Area, where the multiple uses embrace snowmobiles, motorcycles, three-wheeler and four-wheeler ATVs, and 4WDs, a neat little trick of topography frees a long stretch of the ridge from wheels—the only place in the MUA where a pedestrian can be sure of a quiet day.

In Yakima go off US 82/97 on Exit 36 and turn right on Valley Mall

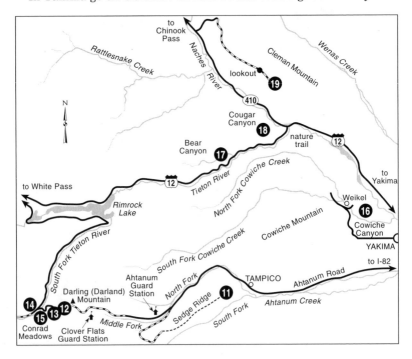

Sedge Ridge

Boulevard into Union Gap. In 0.4 mile from the highway turn right on Main Street; an airplane symbol directs the way toward the Yakima Air Terminal. At 1 mile turn left on Washington Avenue (follow the airplane symbols and signs for "Perry Institute"). Pass the airport and Perry Institute and at 6.2 miles turn left on South 64th, which bends right and merges with Ahtanum Road. At 20.2 miles from the highway is a Y at the fire station and grocery store of Tampico. Take the right fork up North Fork Ahtanum Creek 9.2 miles to a Y. Take the left, Middle Fork Ahtanum Road, 0.3 mile, passing the entry to Ahtanum Camp and Picnic Area, and turn left on road A-2400. Cross the creek 0.1 mile to a quarry, where an alternate road joins from the camp. Turn right, over a cattle guard and past an enormous parking lot (snowmobile staging area). From an elevation of 3200 feet at the quarry, road A-2400 ascends Sedge Ridge, the way narrow but never too steep or rough for the average family car. At 3880 feet, 2.5 miles from Middle Fork Ahtanum Road, is a Y; go left (elsewhere simply ignore the many minor harvesting roads). At 4 miles the road attains the crest of the ridge at an intersection. Park here, elevation 4600 feet.

Walk east straight through the intersection (the left descends to private land and the right follows Sedge Ridge to Darling Mountain) on or

Northern buckwheat on Sedge Ridge

near the crest. The road continues to be possibly drivable by a family car, certainly by any 4WD, but what, then, of the flowers? However, should legions of wheels be on the roll, a person may wish to drive laboriously to the terrain's little trick, the wheel-stop.

The hike may be said to be backwards-front, starting as it does in the Ponderosa Pine Zone, ending in shrub-steppe, the reverse of the usual sequence. The reason is that from Tampico upvalley on both slopes of Sedge Ridge the array of "No Trespassing" signs forbids the public feet—but also the public wheels, and thus the haven of peace.

The way begins in open pine forest carpeted with pinegrass. Patches of steppe commence; sagebrush is scanty but bitterbrush plentiful, as well as snowbrush, the sun baking out its distinctive "*Ceanothus* reek." Flowers are a constant: penstemons, buckwheats, sunflowers, collomia, brodiea, and dozens more. Bitterroot is one of the big stars, scarlet gilia another, and mariposa lily, and the odd seedpods of locoweed. Watch for the unusual blossoms of the rather uncommon clarkia. Views widen; a short side road climbs left to the site of a long-gone fire lookout, 4837 feet.

The crest becomes steppe that is less shrubby than rocky—a fine example of a lithosol. At a scant 2 miles is the alternate parking spot, 4560 feet, where the splendid little trick stops all wheels, appalled as they are by a steep, 400-foot descent through forest to a saddle, 4150 feet. The boulder-blocky tundra turns back machines. Feet, however, find an easy way down an elk trail–cowpath off left below the crest.

To be sure, 4WD tracks resume at the saddle, but faint; few wheels ever climb here, and those solely of cowboys gittin' their little dogies along and local hunters bringing in the family's fall harvest of deer and elk; the tracks ascend from the Tampico vicinity and there are sternly signed "No Trespassing." The crest ascends to Peak 4279, a rounded tundra-like dome, and at a long 2 miles from the good trick reaches Peak 4287, far enough. The views are north to Foundation Ridge and Pine Mountain, south to the long nakedness of Ahtanum Ridge (in the Yakama Indian Reservation), east to the sprawl of Yakima and the broad Yakima Valley, which loses itself in haze on the way to the Columbia River. (Backpackers note: The light show at night is spectacular—city lights, star lights.) What's to the west? Ridges block the view—but behold "beach" sand amid the basalt rocks—St. Helens will not be soon forgotten!

The recommended trip ends here at the edge of public land but the ridge does not, and 2 miles east from Peak 4287 still is at 3700 feet, only then commencing a steep drop to the toe slopes, flower-steppe all the way.

12 DARLING (DARLAND) MOUNTAIN

Length: round trip 5 miles
High point: 6981 feet
Elevation gain: 700 feet (approximate)
Management: Washington Department of Natural Resources
USGS map: Darland Mountain
DNR map: Ahtanum Multiple-Use Area

The maps published by the federals in Washington City or Denver and the state bureaucrats in Olympia say "Darland" but the locals (including the late Supreme Court Justice William O. Douglas) have twisted the name to one that is much more evocative; the mountain truly is a darling, the way it hitches together Sedge Ridge, which rises from a sagebrush valley to subalpine forest, and the Klickton Divide, which proceeds westward and upward to Le Gran Plateau, the Ice Cream Dome, and the glaciers of Mount Gilbert, highest peak of the Goat Rocks. Should the objection be made that a summit as lofty as Darling has no place in a sagebrush book, the answer is that a person walking the steppe has a Muir-like right to know what it's hitched to. Moreover, the mountain does have sagebrush— as well as views of five volcanoes and scores of glaciers, which is what the sagebrush is hitched to.

Darling Mountain

61

Darling Mountain

There is a window of opportunity for the pedestrian in the Ahtanum Multiple-Use Area, the weeks when there's not enough snow for snowmobiles and too much for ATVs. Depending on the elevation and the wintriness of the spring, the window for any one spot is sometime between early April and late June. At the right moment the 3¹⁄₃-mile walk from Tree Phones Camp (4811 feet) to Clover Flats (6320 feet) can be both brilliantly flowerful and idyllically peaceful. For the darling itself the window usually opens in late May and remains open until near the end of June; a midweek hiker can find quiet even later.

From the North Fork–Middle Fork Y at Ahtanum Camp and Picnic Area (see Hike 11) drive Middle Fork Ahtanum Road 5.7 miles to Tree Phones Camp and 3.3 miles more to Clover Flats Scenic Camp. Park here, elevation 6320 feet. Park sooner if snowbanks dictate. Or, if the snow is all melted, drive on—the road continues to the very summit, rather rude yet easy enough for a moderately tough family car. But it's such a bully walk!

The road makes a stiff bit of a climb from the lush green meadows of Clover Flats, bright in snowmelt season with glacier lily, spring beauty, buttercup, and marsh marigold, across a hillside of subalpine fir to a plateau ashed gray by St. Helens, gardened to a dusty barren by gophers. In 1¹/₂ miles is a Y, 6779 feet. The left, signed "Klickitat Meadows," runs west along Sedge Ridge (see Hike 11). The right, signed "Darland Mountain" (sic!), drops a bit to a saddle, the slopes draining left to the Klickitat River, right into Greens Pocket and North Fork Ahtanum Creek. The final mile is through meadows featuring a gallery of white pine and whitebark pine, living trees tortured by winds into handsome green sculptures, lightning-killed trees bleached by the elements into silver sculptures. The flowers are profusely subalpine—yet there is some sagebrush, too, both big and dwarf.

The summit plateau, 6981 feet, is extensive. A huge readerboard affirms the identity of "Darling Mountain." For the best views walk to the edge, where pine sculptures don't block out Hood, Adams, the remnants of St. Helens, and Rainier. The fifth volcano? You're standing near the middle of it—the middle of where it was, as bulky and tall a mass as Adams. The roots remain—the Goat Rocks Wilderness. To the north are Aix and other peaks of the William O. Douglas Wilderness. East, beyond the long thrust of Sedge Ridge, is Yakima. Look, as well, straight down to the South Fork Tieton River and Conrad Meadows (see Hike 15).

13 BLUE SLIDE LOOKOUT

Length: round trip 6 miles
High point: 6785 feet
Elevation gain: 2300 feet
Management: Wenatchee National Forest and Washington Department of Natural Resources
USGS map: Darland Mountain
DNR map: Ahtanum Multiple-Use Area

The lookout cabin of old was perched on the tip of a rock promontory jutting way out there in the middle of the air, high above the Tieton River concordance of valleys. Long gone, of course. But the outlook still is the grandest any lookout in these parts ever had. White Pass Highway can be traced from Central Washington sagebrush past Rimrock Reservoir to the Cascade Crest. North of the pass is the William O. Douglas Wilderness, named for the Supreme Court justice who practically invented wilderness; south, the Goat Rocks Wilderness. The most startling scenery, though, is not out there but straight down to the valley, wherefrom rise the anomalous mound of Goose Egg Mountain and the mythic lava crags of Kloochman Rock.

In his books Justice Douglas wrote of boyhood rambles through all this Tieton–Ahtanum–Klickitat country. Tragically, his trails have been conceded without so much as a skirmish to the hordes of SUVs, 4WDs (4x4 jeeps), ORVs, and ATVs, the multiple-abusers tolerated—nay, benignly fostered—by their acronymic siblings, the USFS and DNR. Before a just share of the unique geography can be restored to exclusive use of feet and hooves, a new generation of nonmechanicals must rediscover the land of the Douglas youth. The task can be undertaken now, and joyously, free from racket and turmoil of the toy-boys, in midweek. Best of all is early summer, when bare ground between snowpatches turns back snowmobiles while the snowpatches turn back wheels.

Drive US 12 east from White Pass to just short of Hause Creek Campground and turn right on South Fork Tieton Road, doubling back

Talus of basalt rubble on Blue Slide Ridge

westward beside Rimrock Reservoir. At 4.5 miles from the highway turn left on road No. 1000, signed "Conrad Meadows." In 8.5 miles from the turn go left on road No. 1050 and ascend 3.8 miles to a switchback at the lip of the Blue Slide canyon. A short bit past the switchback a gravel fan spilling onto the road identifies the former trail, now "4WD." Elevation, 4500 feet.

The 4WD track climbs steep forest, passing rock outcrops exhaling fragrance of sage and pennyroyal, bits of telephone wire recalling when this was the main horse trail from the Tieton to the lookout. At 5550 feet the ridge narrows to a cleaver edging the Blue Slide canyon, where volcanic trash busted loose and WHOOSHed to the valley.

At the canyon top the 4WD track quits, yielding to genuine trail which soon drops off the ridge into a dandy little meadow basin bounded on one side by a lava talus from a lava bluff and on the other by a heap of moss-greened lava rubble hypothesized to be, perhaps, a relict "rock glacier."

Blue Slide Lookout site

Snow scraps linger to early summer, meltwater rippling by groves of subalpine fir, over fields of glacier lily, polemonium, pussy-paws, buckwheat, partridgefoot, and a world of other color, the more vivid for the contrast of black lava from the Goat Rocks Volcano and companion vents.

The trail intersects a 4WD track ("road No. 621," the shame of it!) which finishes the climb to a 6300-foot saddle in forest atop Divide Ridge. In every direction run 4WDs—east along Divide Ridge into the Ahtanum drainage, southerly along Divide Ridge past 6202-foot Blue Lake to Darling Mountain. The myriad intersections can be confusing, but not terminally befuddling if you keep wits and map about you. Any of several obvious ways by 4WD and/or elk path and/or open forest and steppe meadow lead to the bare rock jut, 6785 feet.

Hark! On a day chosen wisely, hear only winds and birds and silence. Look out to the ridges, down to the valleys, through the eyes of young Bill Douglas to that good past before a Yakima lad's rite of passage was getting his wheels.

14   NARROW NECK GAP

Length: round trip 5 miles
High point: 6480 feet
Elevation gain: 1730 feet
Management: Wenatchee National Forest and Washington Department of
   Natural Resources
USGS map: Darland Mountain
Green Trails map: Rimrock
DNR map: Ahtanum Multiple-Use Area

The geography hereabouts is a fascinating melange of volcanic absurdities. The Blue Slide, for example, and—all along Divide Ridge to Darling Mountain—picturesquely peculiar lava cliffs and felsenmeers

Meadow near Narrow Neck Gap

and taluses, as well as mysterious mounds suspected of being "rock glaciers" left over from the Little Ice Age. —And then, just past Darling Mountain, there's that abrupt notch in the otherwise shoulder-broad crest of Klickton Divide. The obvious explanation is that a band of weak rock offered easy digging by Discovery Creek and Coyote Creek, their canyons on opposite sides of the ridge meeting at the top in that ridiculously skinny neck. These sideshows are amusing. But the center rings are (1) the outlook to volcanoes along the Cascade Crest and to valleys and ridges extending east beyond the reach of Pacific Ocean clouds into the rainshadow sagebrush and (2) my oh my, the sun-country flowers. To see them at their best (and in the season of peace between snowmobiles and wheel-monkeys) come in early summer.

Drive road No. 1000 from Rimrock Reservoir (see Hike 13) 13.5 miles and turn left on road No. 1070. Cross the river and ascend about 1 mile, passing logging spurs, to a junction. Go left on road No. 578 a scant 1 mile to the gash, uphill from the road, of an unsigned (though variously numbered and named on various maps) 4WD track. Elevation, 4750 feet.

The wheel-eroded gash climbs straight up open forest, crosses a closed logging spur, passes bits of telephone wire from the Golden Age, and at 5600 feet swings into, and out of, the swale of a meltwater-time tributary to Discovery Creek. Supersteep wheelway emerges from big-tree forest to steppe-meadow, to pointy-top subalpine firs, feathery-needled larch, and witchy tangles of whitebark pine—and to blossoms. Bitterroot! Buckwheat! Larkspur, wallflower, roseroot, and a glory more.

The angle eases in rolling meadows atop Klickton Divide, the views down to Tieton and Klickitat valleys, out to Mount Adams, Goat Rocks, peaks of the William O. Douglas Wilderness, and Mount Rainier. Though the route is signed as an official ATV route, toy-boys don't get up here much.

Flowers and tree-shrubs and views never quit. At 6480 feet is Narrowneck Knoll. A lover's leap below is that weird Gap, 6400 feet, and a stone's throw beyond begin the slopes of Darling Mountain (Hike 12). Views from its 6981-foot summit are not worth the additional walking because the plateauness of the summit makes them inferior to those of the Knoll.

Press the button on your time machine and see the lad, Bill Douglas, loping from his Yakima home up Ahtanum Creek, over the top of Darling, and down to the Tieton (on the track you have just climbed), and up from Conrad Meadows to summits of the Goat Rocks. When lingering snowfields seasonally transform 4WD gashes of the present to the trails he walked, wander lonely as a cloud, no sounds louder than winds and birds, past Darling Mountain to Blue Slide Lookout (Hike 13) or Sedge Ridge (Hike 11), or along Klickton Divide to Spencer Point and Petross Sidehill, where wheel scars fade out in old-timey foot-only meadows. Search for traces of the ancient Klickitat Trail to Cispus Pass.

15 CONRAD MEADOWS

Length: round trip 3 miles
High point: 4000 feet
Elevation gain: none
Management: Wenatchee National Forest
USGS maps: White Pass, Walupt Lake

The largest valley-bottom midmontane meadow in the Cascades doesn't get any respect. A person must travel to Montana to find the likes of Conrad Meadows, yet Wenatchee National Forest resolutely refuses to recognize the ecological uniqueness, continues to permit cows to crop and flop the hundreds of acres of flowers, refuses to acquire the private lands that ought to be placed in the Goat Rocks Wilderness. As with Darling Mountain, which stands on high above the

South Tieton River and Conrad Meadows

meadows, the question may be asked, What's this trip doing in this book? Again the answer is, To make the connection. Sagebrush does, in fact, reach to the east portion of the meadows; leaving it behind, and looking up to the glaciers on the Goat Rocks, finishes the job started by Darling—the walker gets hitched.

From Rimrock Reservoir drive road No. 1000 (see Hike 13) 14 miles to a gate at the edge of private property. Park hereabouts, elevation 3900 feet.

South Fork Tieton trail No. 1120 passes the gate, then fords Short Creek and Long Creek, to a Y. Take the left, the Ten Day Creek trail, along the meadow edge beside the river. In a short bit the path drops to a ford. Don't cross. Proceed upstream near the riverbank on intermittent elk trail–cowpath. The way is partly in dry meadow blossoming in agoseris, lupine, strawberry, Jacobs ladder, groundsel, sunflower, yarrow, desert parsley, cinquefoil, clover, pussytoes, vetch, phlox, wandering daisy; in wet meadows of littleflower penstemon, camas, sidalcea, thistle, larkspur, speedwell, violet, bistort, spring beauty, paintbrush, alpine veronica, meadow parsley, forget-me-not; and in boggy meadows of elephanthead, white bog orchid, buttercup, monkeyflower, hellebore. The flowering begins in April, runs through its repertoire until July— and then the cows arrive and that's that.

Blackbirds scold, swallows swoop, nutcrackers squawk. Small raptors explode from the grass. A fox lopes across the meadow. The river runs milky from the rock-milling of Conrad Glacier. Beside it are heaps of St. Helens ash, prevented from forming dunes only by the constant trampling of the elk.

In 1 long mile riparian brush forces the walker away from the river; vast mush-meadows of tall grass and sedge and over-the-shoes water then induce him to seek higher ground, attained on private land where lodgepole pine was logged in the 1970s. Here the trail is intersected and can be walked upstream to the last of the valley-bottom meadows at 4 miles, 4250 feet. However, the main extent of Conrad Meadows ends at the logging. Turn back downvalley, through the center of the flatland, anciently a lakebed. From groves of white-gleaming aspen look back up to the white-gleaming glaciers on Mount Gilbert.

Lupine

16 COWICHE CANYON CONSERVANCY

Length: round trip 3 miles
High point: 1550 feet
Elevation gain: on return 250 feet
Management: Cowiche Canyon Conservancy
USGS maps: Naches, Wiley City, Yakima West

Birds warble in the willow and red-osier dogwood along Cowiche Creek. Flowers brighten crannies in the basalt walls and colorfully slash the sagebrush hills—the purple sage particularly a joy in late May. Famous though the canyon is for rattlesnakes, fear not—the trail is wide and open, reptiles easy to see and avoid. The reason the trail is so wide is that it was built by the Northern Pacific Railroad, twisting through the sinuous canyon on a typically easy grade, 100 feet of elevation differential per mile. No need to keep a lookout for trains—they've been gone for years. No need to fret about other traffic, either—in establishing the Cowiche Canyon Conservancy, Yakima County ruled out

Cowiche Canyon

wheels and the trail is gated against all manner of motors.

Driving US 12 west through Yakima, at North 40th Avenue and Fruitvale Exit cross Fruitvale Boulevard and go south on North 40th 1.4 miles. Turn right on Summitview Road 7 miles. At a large log house turn right on Weikel Road 0.5 mile, then right again at the former Weikel Station, and in 0.2 mile reach the trailhead, elevation 1550 feet.

In a scant ¼ mile cross Cowiche Creek on the first of six bridges. The canyon walls rise 200 feet from the trail, an interesting mix of gray shale and large basalt columns, some a brilliant brick-red. At about 1¼ miles, having along the way gone through a deep cut and crossed those six bridges, the railroad came to a seventh bridge. But it's presently missing, as are the eighth and ninth bridges. In the high water of spring the choice is between turning around or

Magpie

wading. In the low water of summer the creek can be hopped across on hopping stones, extending the trip 1½ miles to the first house, elevation 1300 feet.

Though the Cowiche Canyon Trail is a wildland walk and the start of human habitations signals a turnaround for wildlanders, eventually the route will connect to the 4.6-mile Yakima Greenway, an urban trail.

17 BEAR CANYON

Length: round trip 2 to 5 miles
High point: 3400 feet
Elevation gain: 1200 feet
Management: Wenatchee National Forest
USGS map: Weddle Canyon

A washout in 1980 or so gave pedestrians a footroad that winds through a narrow defile. Canyon walls and valley-bottom trees help the hiker keep cool. Until early summer, when the creek quits, a

Slopes above Bear Canyon

splendid backpacker camp is well watered. Then comes the climb to the high ridges, the broad views.

Drive US 12 east from White Pass to a few feet short of milepost 179, the Wenatchee National Forest boundary sign, and the Bear Creek road going off left. If coming east from Yakima, see the sign saying "Entering Oak Creek Wildlife Recreation Area." Follow the road uphill 0.4 mile to the washout and trailhead, elevation 2200 feet.

Step across Bear Creek (easy) and walk a sometimes-smooth road-bed and a sometimes-rubbly trail. Canyon walls. Trees. In season, a creek. At 1³/₄ miles, near an old gravel pit, is an excellent campsite. Here is the first easy route up the open slopes to the right, which are south-facing and thus the sunniest and the driest and most open, which means the floweriest the earliest. So that's one trip.

The other, with the broadest views, heads for the ridge on the left, whose slopes face north and thus are the shadiest and wettest, which means they are forested and the latest to flower. For these slopes, continue up the canyon. At about 3 miles reach road No. 1401. (This road, which appears to be 4WD-negotiable, comes from the Bethel Ridge road, starting near the Oak Creek Wildlife headquarters.) Go left and up, climbing from Bear Creek in trees ½ mile, and then turn left up a cat road to the opens and the views on the crest, 3400 feet.

18 NACHES RIVER– COUGAR CANYON

Length: round trip 2 to 6 miles
High point: 800 or 3100 feet (approximate)
Elevation gain: 150 or 1500 feet (approximate)
Management: State Wildlife Department
USGS maps: Tieton, Milk Creek

A wide bench above the Naches River provides an easy and delightful walk through flowers on the valley wall. A trail extends onward to the mouth of Cougar Canyon, solitude guaranteed—on *this* side of the river; across the waters, just a stone's throw away, are vehicles on US 410. But don't throw stones. From your citadel of peace, pity those folks who know not how to move about the earth except on wheels.

Drive north from Naches on US 12 to the junction with US 410. Keep left on US 12, crossing the Naches River. Immediately beyond the bridge turn right into an access to the Oak Creek Wildlife Recreation Area. Since this is the wintering range of the elk herds, in spring a visitor may see hundreds of the animals. The trail starts at the end of the road, elevation 1650 feet.

Walk ½ mile up the Naches valley to an unusual and awkward but very effective gate in the elk fence. A service road follows the fence a scant 1 mile to a high overlook of river and mountains on a terrace

Above: *Early spring elk herd at Oak Creek Wildlife Recreation Area.*
Below: *Naches River Trail.*

where the river flowed in ancient times. Find a soft patch of ground and get out the peanut butter and celery.

If more of a trip is wanted, continue about ½ mile to where the road descends to a gate and private property. Stay on WRA land, close to the fence, on smatterings of old 4WD track that proceed upriver another ¾ mile. Where the route dips to river level, spot an obscure trail through the brush to the mouth of Cougar Canyon and an idyllic picnic scene about 2¼ miles from the car.

For a couple of hours of truly pure solitude, climb the 3100-foot hill (the lower end of Bethel Ridge) above Cougar Canyon and walk the ridge east to the starting point.

19 CLEMAN MOUNTAIN

Length: round trip 1 to 20 miles
High point: 5115 feet
Elevation gain: none to 3200 feet (approximate)
Management: State Wildlife Department
USGS map: Milk Creek

Is it steppe? Or arctic tundra? Or mountain meadow? With elevations that top out at 5115 feet, Cleman Mountain is the quintessence of "desert-alpine." From a distance the long ridge appears stark naked; actually the canyons of the northeast slope nurture strip forests, and the springs that dot the smoother southwest slope feed lush clumps of greenery. On the crest, too, wherever a swale or knob gives some protection from the sun, there are huddlings of pine and subalpine fir. However, the dominant character of the mountain is wide-open space, miles and miles on top of the world with views down to valleys of the Naches and Wenas and Yakima, out to Rainier, Adams, Goat Rocks, and where—until 1980—St. Helens showed the tip of its white cone above the Cascade Crest.

Cleman is laced with 4WD roads from the North Wenas Valley, few suitable for a family car, all excellent footroads. But then, in this sort of terrain the foot can go where it will and where wheels never do; trails are a luxury, not a necessity. Local hikers simply strike off up the slope from US 410 near the junction with US 12, gaining 3200 feet to the crest. A less strenuous alternative starting from the valley is the Mud Lake road, gaining 1500 feet. The favorite is a start from the crest, leaving the climbing to the machine, saving for the feet the relaxed fun of rambling the ridge.

Drive US 410 to 18 miles west of Naches. Between mileposts 104 and 103 turn right on Forest Service road No. 1701, signed "Bald Mountain" and "Rocky Flat." Pass road No. 1711 and at 4.8 miles from the highway reach the ridge top and a junction, elevation 3800 feet. Road No. 1701 goes left towards Bald Mountain and meadows to roam. Go right on

View from Cleman Mountain

road No. 1712, signed "Cleman Mountain L.P. 7 miles." The track deteriorates but is passable (most of the way, anyhow) by the average family car. (If not by yours, remember the nice gravel road towards Bald Mountain.) Park near the lookout site, elevation 5115 feet.

If views are the goal, just sit in the car and soak them up. Terrific. They don't get any better afoot. But you can't stick your nose in a flower while perched atop four wheels or even two. So get out and walk, mingling the all-around-horizon views with the all-around gardens. Follow the ups and downs of the crest southeast towards the 4924-foot knoll overlooking the Yakima Valley, some 5 miles from the lookout. Or stop shorter or go farther. Feel free.

Umtanum East

Yakima River from Skyline Rim Trail

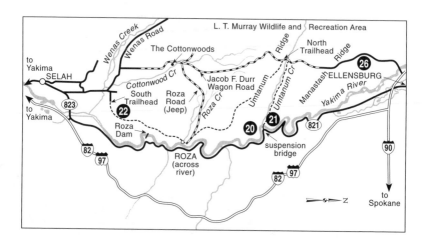

20   YAKIMA RIVER VIEW

Length: round trip 2 to 4 miles
High point: 1950 feet (approximate)
Elevation gain: 600 feet (approximate)
Management: State Wildlife Department
USGS map: Wymer

Umtanum Ridge pushes out east from the Cascades to the Yakima
River—and, indeed, beyond, because in the geologic past, as ridges rose
in east–west lines across its course, the north–south river kept cutting
down, slicing the great canyon of the Yakima. The feature of this hike
is the vertical view down these canyon walls to the river flowing sinu-
ously through intrenched meanders.

Drive Canyon Road (SR 821) between Ellensburg and Yakima. Between mileposts 16 and 17 (these mark the distance from the Yakima
end) is the Umtanum Creek Recreation Area. Park near the suspension bridge, elevation 1340 feet.

Cross the river on the foot-only suspension bridge, cross the railroad
tracks, in a few feet pass a fence, then a thicket, and in a small clear-
ing, about 200 feet from the river, go left on a faint path which in
another 200 feet turns right on an old bulldozer track that skirts the
base of a steep slope. The track becomes steep, darn steep, as it
makes a sidehilling ascent into a tributary valley. At about 1/2 mile is a
junction with a road that is not too rough for 4WDs. To the right it
climbs the ridge to Durr Road (Hike 22). Go left and up to the ridge
top, 1950 feet.

Spectacular! The river runs 600 feet below; install a springboard and the high-diving would be world-class. For more views and flowers, continue on the 4WD track 1½ miles, dipping to a second stupendous vista.

Yakima River and footbridge, Umtanum Creek Recreation Area

21 UMTANUM CANYON

Length: round trip 4 to 6 miles
High point: 1500 feet (approximate)
Elevation gain: 200 feet (approximate)
Management: State Wildlife Department
USGS maps: Wymer, Ellensburg

The Yakima River Canyon is scenic on the big scale, appropriately famous, and the highway is deservedly thronged. The tributary Umtanum Creek Canyon is equally scenic on a more intimate scale, is inappropriately obscure, and the trail is happily lonesome, known only to those plucky pedestrians not scared off by the nickname, "Rattlesnake Alley."

Because there is water and riparian greenery there notably are snakes. Sorry to say, the flowers of spring blossom only after the reptiles emerge from hibernation, and the fangs remain a menace when

Beaver logger at work

the groves of cottonwood and aspen flame golden yellow in the fall sun. However, as this book's introduction explains, they are too much feared by visitors from the poison-free side of the Cascades. Nevertheless, the nervous are reminded that in winter there are no snakes around. And the scenery is as fine as in other seasons.

Drive Canyon Road (SR 821) to the Umtanum Creek Recreation Area (see Hike 20), elevation 1340 feet. Cross the foot-only suspension bridge, cross the railroad tracks, and find the trail where it enters a thicket. The way follows Umtanum Creek over a broad meadow and through orchards abandoned perhaps half a century ago, the trees so gnarled as to be scarcely recognizable for what they are until a lonesome apple is spotted.

At about ¾ mile the trail forks. The left is a dead end. Go right across the creek, via a wade in early spring, dry-foot stepping stones later. At about 1½ miles the creek bottom appears to have been clearcut; inspection reveals it definitely has been logged—by beavers.

Wide enough at the start for orchards, at 2 miles the valley abruptly narrows to a genuine canyon; at 3 miles it is a claustrophobic cleft. Day hikers generally prefer a turnaround hereabouts. Backpackers find a number of attractive camps beside the cheerful bubbling of the creek. The trail continues to Durr Road (Hike 22).

22 YAKIMA RIM SKYLINE TRAIL

Management: State Wildlife Department
USGS maps: Badger Pocket, Ellensburg, Yakima East, Selah

When word got around in 1977 that the Wildlife (then, Game) Department had built a 15-mile trail along the ridges above the renowned Yakima Canyon, pedestrians went as berserk as America's wastrels and drifters when gold was found at Sutter's Mill. Hikers whose boots knew only forests and meadows and snowfields, who were convinced you sang about but didn't walk about the lone prairie where the coyotes howl and the wind blows free, stampeded the instant classic of the "end-to-end" through the "desert-alpine" gardens of bitterroot and cactus and a glory more, under the "house of sky" where the prairie falcons and golden eagles and kestrels and redtail hawks sail the thermals and swoop down to snatch lunch from the sagebrush.

Why these two decades later is the treasure trove next to deserted? Did the treasure run out? By no means. The 100,000-acre L. T. Murray Wildlife Recreation Area, acquired in 1968, preserves wildlife habitat better than ever, and the Game/Wildlife Department's first-ever recreational trail, deliberately designed for "nonconsumptive" recreation, is sure to last a geologic epoch or so even with no maintenance

Roza Dam, railroad bridge, and Yakima River from Skyline Rim Trail

whatsoever. However, due to departmental neglect (lack of funds), the situation is now so messy that nobody much even tries the classic "end-to-end" anymore.

Herein, therefore, we introduce the new classic, which in our opinion is even classier. Directions also are included for the end-to-end, though the 15 miles have become more like 18, plus a 4-mile roundtrip sidetrip up Roza Creek to fill waterbags at Birdsong Spring, the only potable water anywhere near the route.

There are still, as before, three trailheads, all served by Durr Road, which requires a section all to itself.

Jacob Durr Road

Driving from the south: Go off I-90 on Exit 109 and drive Canyon Road (SR 821) through the Yakima Canyon to the Selah exit. Go off onto Harrison Road (at this point, not signed) 1.9 miles to a T intersection. Turn right on North Wenas Road 2.8 miles to a Y at a fire station. For the *South Trailhead,* go right, straight ahead, on Gibson Road.

To proceed north, stay on North Wenas Road 1.8 miles past the fire station and turn off right on Sheep Company Road. Pavement ceases, a sign erroneously warns "Dead End," and at 1.4 miles from North Wenas Road is the entry to the L. T. Murray WRA. The road instantly dwindles as it changes name (though no sign at this point says so) to the Jacob F. Durr Wagon Road, a toll road that served as the pioneer route linking Yakima and Ellensburg in the 1880s. The "sheep company" operated hereabouts for decades, and in the 1920s Gibson and his cowboys ran a herd of buffalo (bison from Yellowstone) on the range. The Wildlife Department, while enhancing wildlife habitat by closing most old wagon–jeep tracks to public

Sunflowers

wheels, posts green-dot markers denoting routes that can be legally driven. Durr Road is one of these. Maintenance, mostly by utilities (electricity, natural gas), is adequate for service trucks; occupants of passenger vehicles will travel much of the way with clenched teeth, now and then opening them to emit little shrieks of alarm or outright terror.

At 2.5 miles from the L. T. Murray boundary Durr Road crosses Cottonwood Creek to a triple fork. The left is unsigned, the middle "To Ridge," and the right "Durr Road." In 0.1 mile more is another Y, elevation 1850 feet. The left is signed "Durr." The unsigned right is Roza Road to the *Middle (Roza) Trailhead.*

Roza Road–Durr Road proceeds 5.2 miles to the head of the Cottonwood Creek valley and steeply, roughly to the crest of Umtanum Ridge, 3375 feet. (It is not considered sissy to park and walk the last couple of miles. After all, the flowers are as great here as anywhere.) At a Y just short of the crest, the left climbs to a microwave tower atop Peak 3618 (a good little walk in its own right); Durr Road contours a short bit to a cattleguard and begins the descent to Umtanum Creek. Here is the *North Trailhead.*

Driving from the north: Go off I-90 on Exit 109, turn north 0.6 mile on Canyon Road, and turn left (west) on Dammon Road. At Dammon

School, 1.7 miles from Canyon Road, is a four-way intersection. The straight-through road, Dammon (or "Damman") to this point, changes name to Umtanum ("Umptanum"). At the far side of the Kittitas Valley floor it abruptly ascends little Shushuskin Canyon. At 5 miles from Canyon Road go left off the paved road onto the unpaved and probably unsigned Durr Road. Proceed across the high plateau to the end of farmhouses and plowed fields, pass a side road off east, and clench teeth to commence the steep, narrow, rough descent to the floor of Umtanum Canyon. If you meet oncoming traffic on a switchback, shriek once and die. At 4.1 miles from Umtanum Road is the ford of Umtanum Creek, a good trick if you come too early in spring. A 3-mile climb, for a total 12.1 miles from Umtanum Road, culminates at the *North Trailhead.*

Walking from the South Trailhead

Length: round trip from 1996 de facto south trailhead to Roza Valley overlook 14 miles
High point: 3000 feet
Elevation gain: (going and coming) 3000 feet

At the fire-station Y on North Wenas Road, go right, straight ahead, 0.3 mile on Gibson Road and turn right on Buffalo Road. In 0.5 mile is an "End of County Road" sign, and in another 1.2 miles the last in a series of "No Trespassing" signs, this one enforced by a locked gate in a fence crossable only if you have the wings of an angel. In 1 more mile is the Old Abandoned South Trailhead, 1300 feet, 2.7 miles from Gibson Road. You can't drive there because the Wildlife Department neglected to get easements for the access road and the residents ultimately wearied of the Saturday night wild and crazy guys flinging beer cans and shooting guns in all directions.

It would be a pity to utterly give up on this southern segment of the old classic. Aside from preserving the possibility of the end-to-end (hoping the Wildlife Department might someday resuscitate its noble concept), the low elevation and the short distance from a county road easily passable the year-around enable an enchantment of flower-walking while higher ridges are still winter-dun. Moreover, this is the most quintessentially canyonesque stretch of the route, beginning at the mouth of the Yakima Canyon on the boundary between creeping suburbia and open-range highlands and climbing the ridge exactly on the rim, lava ramparts plummeting to the Yakima River.

The new (temporary?) 1996 trailhead is at a sharp right turn at that "End of County Road" sign, elevation 1300 feet, 0.5 mile from Gibson Road. All along here an elk drift fence keeps elk in and hikers out of the WRA. Just past the sharp right turn is an indent in the fence to provide a spacious parking area. From it, an open-to-the-feet gate allows pedestrian entry into the WRA.

Though the lack of formal tread makes for some stumbling here and there, the route to the trail is self-evident. In the 2½ pathless miles, ascending along the drift fence to 1600 feet or so, the flowers of late March and early April may well be enough to make a full day's trip. Intersecting the trail is inevitable; the tall route-marking posts set securely in the ground are visible from great distances, and after 20 years only several have fallen.

Once the tread is attained, the walking scarcely ever veers from the big-view rim, ascending from one false summit to the next, vistas swelling south to Wenas Valley and Selah, east to the big noises of the military's Yakima Firing Center. Peak 2737 is topped, overlooking Roza Dam and bugs creeping Canyon Road, 1500 vertical feet below. The trail drops to a 2500-foot saddle, climbs and drops again, then dips briefly from the crest to Twin Springs, 2525 feet. The jungle of serviceberry, bitter cherry, creek dogwood, currant, Oregon grape, mock orange, and other shrubs has the only plants on the route taller than sagebrush. The two tanks may or may not have water in them, and it

Interstate 82 from south Skyline Rim Trail

may or may not be humanly potable, but the wildlife mightily appreciate washing down the food they crop from the cafeteria grove. The water-cooled shade is a splendid opportunity to study rattlesnakes.

The ascent resumes, regaining the ridge crest and sidehilling Peak 3208 to the high point of the southern segment of the trail, 3000 feet, a very satisfying turnaround for a day hike, though considerably more strenuous than in days of yore. Note how the broad valley of Roza Creek on one side of the river is matched on the other by the broad Burbank Valley. Visualize the Umtanum Anticline pushing the old lava flows upward, folding them, and the river maintaining its course, cutting ever downward.

Walking from the North Trailhead

Length: round trip to Peak 3375 6 miles
Elevation gain: 600 feet going, 600 feet coming

This is far and away the most-walked part of the trail, for several reasons. The crest of Umtanum Ridge rolls along high in the sky, the ups and downs so minor, and the winds so cooling, a hiker has to go

Lost sign at north trailhead

Abandoned building on Skyline Rim Trail

at a run to break a sweat. The views extend from the glaciers of Mount Rainier and Mount Adams in the south to the crags of the Stuart Range in the north. Though the route is some distance removed from the Yakima Canyon rim, immediately below is the slot of Umtanum Canyon, no mean gash in its own right. Flowers? In May entire hillsides are so white with phlox a person wonders if there was a sneaky overnight snowfall. Several species of buckwheat patchwork acres of tundra in hues from white to bright yellow to pink. Desert parsley and wallflower and a variety of sunflowers yellow the crest, larkspur and lupine and penstemon and brodiea and mertensia and onion add shades of blue to violet. Bitterroot! Both species of cactus native to Washington!

The walk out and back is an easy day for children. The backpacking is popular—load water and root beer on the back, carry a little stove or sup on sandwiches and nibbles, and throw down the sleeping bag in any of the many private nooks. Watch the sun go down, the stars and the lights of farms and cities sparkle out, the sun come up.

Let the feet loose—they can't go wrong. The ridge top undulates to the highest point of the Skyline Trail, 3550 feet, location of a microwave reflector and the ruins of an old shack. Peak 3375 is a suggested turnaround, but feel free.

Walking from the Middle (Roza) Trailhead

At the 1850-foot Y where Durr Road goes left, go right on the gully-ruts of unsigned Roza Road, gasping in disbelief that it merits the green dot signifying official roadness. No ignominy attaches to walking rather than driving up the pleasant draw to the height of land between Cottonwood and Roza Creeks, 2260 feet, at 2.4 miles reaching the end of green-dot approval, a sign proclaiming the road-that-was must have

Roza Dam and Yakima River

Seldom-seen badger

"No unauthorized use beyond this point." This, then, is the new Middle (Roza) Trailhead, elevation 2100 feet.

Here begins the New Classic: A short backpack to the sweetest camp this side of Heaven, base for two day hikes south and north from Roza Creek to the big-sky views, and so home with a 3-day birdbag of ravens, magpies, meadowlarks, chats, orioles, doves, swallows, rock wrens, and one of the densest raptor populations in the state, a chance to see coyotes, bobcats, and bighorn sheep or at least their scat, and— oh boy—the flowers that bloom in the spring, tra-la-la-la.

The disauthorization of the road down Roza Creek has eliminated the mindless buzzing about of the 4WDs and SUVs and ATVs, and an invasive alien yellow-flowering species of the Pea Family has so obscured the track that scofflaw wheels are daunted by the challenges that cannot be seen from the driver's seat. On a fine spring day of 1996 no wheel prints of any kind were to be seen, only prints of animals and boots. Peace!

At 1¼ miles from the trailhead is Birdsong Camp, 1700 feet. Cool, sweet water trickles through a lushness of roses and speedwell and monkeyflower and all, birds twittering and sipping and rattlesnakes chilling out. The giant, old, gnarled locust planted by the long-ago homesteaders (house foundations can be found) has two young scions to perpetuate the species, apple trees still cling to life, and the water-loving native trees and shrubs and herbs exuberate. At dawn's first

Birdsong Tree near Roza Creek

light the wings arrive from miles around to strike up the band. No deep sleep, here, under the spreading Birdsong Tree, not until dusk, when nighthawks and bats eclipse the stars, and the loudest sounds are crickets and coyotes.

South from Birdsong

Length: round trip from Birdsong to 3000-foot high point 9½ miles
Elevation gain: (going and coming) 2100 feet

The walk begins with 2 miles on the road-become-trail down Roza Creek to the stone foundation of Roza School, the skeleton of a box-elder in whose shadows students once played, and the intersection,

1300 feet, with the Yakima Rim Skyline Trail.

There is no trailhead sign, nor for the first part any visible tread, but route-marking posts guide the feet south across the broad gravel wash of Roza Creek, dry by late spring but obviously a terror in snowmelt or cloudbursts. Meager tread angles off leftward to the toe of the slope, passes through a barbed-wire fence to another post, and crosses a shallow draw to an old road; a pair of posts inform the hiker not to go left or right on it but straight across.

Plain trail ascends to a hogback that rises from riverbank and railroad. The rim is quickly attained in grand views down to meanders of the river and to Selah Butte in the lava-rampart stretch of canyon beyond Roza Dam. The scenery expands as the path ascends the rim to the trail's high point of 3000 feet. Turning

Meadowlark

back here is not mandatory; the flowers continue, better and better.

Indeed, on one of those elysian days when cool breezes don't let you feel your sunburn until after sunset, it's just about mandatory to continue to Twin Springs, 2525 feet, and Peak 2737, overlooking the canyon's south portal, though these add 4 miles and 800 feet to the round trip.

To resurrect a segment of the old end-to-end, the one-way distance from the Middle (Roza) Trailhead to the de facto South Trailhead is about 13½ miles, not a hard day if a friend is there to give a pick-up.

North from Birdsong

Length: round trip from Birdsong to Peak 3375 14 miles
Elevation gain: (going and coming) 2500 feet

The trail can readily be found in the tall grass beside the road near the schoolhouse. Posts lead around a corner of a footing ridge close above the river. A dry gulch interrupts the tread. Go downstream a bit on abandoned road and find a resumption of the trail, climbing from the gulch and switchbacking up a steep slope. The posts quit, no longer needed, the tread distinct and the crest of Umtanum Ridge impossible to miss.

The way reaches the rocky brink overlooking the river and follows the exact crest of the ridge to Peak 2400, where two pairs of posts mark an old (now forbidden) wheel route. Tread hereabouts is so meager the traces of road are the easier walking to Peak 2700, where the old wheel route makes a T with a newer one that retains green-dot approval, and that's a crying shame. Views are across the valley of the Yakima River, here wide and with a floodplain, to the heights of Baldy. The way undulates, up a bit, down a bit, to Peak 3250, Peak 3320, and Peak 3370, the same elevation as the North Trailhead, which is not far. But for this trip, why go on? Return to the wheelfree seclusion of Roza Creek and the melodious camp under the spreading Birdsong Tree.

As for the old end-to-end, the one-way distance from the Middle (Roza) Trailhead to the North Trailhead is about 12 miles, not bad if a friend is there with wheels.

Umtanum West

Buckwheat blooming above Hardy Canyon

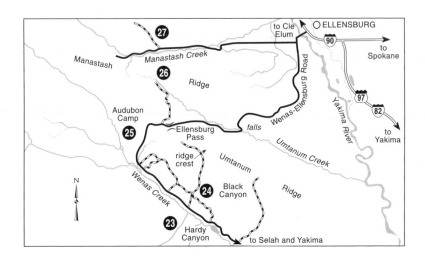

23 HARDY CANYON

Length: round trip 1 to 6 miles
High point: 3500 feet (approximate)
Elevation gain: 500 to 1100 feet (approximate)
Management: State Wildlife Department
USGS maps: Wenas Lake, Milk Canyon

As viewed from green fields of the irrigated Wenas Valley, the enclosing ridges appear to be stark-naked desert. True enough, there are miles of wide-open ridges to walk where grass and flowers and sagebrush are the tallest vegetation, nothing to block the broad vistas down to farms and out to the Cascades. However, in the canyons there are also wet meadows, swamps, marshes, and groves of cottonwood, aspen, wild cherry, serviceberry, and "just plain brush." A rough and tough road can be walked, perhaps driven, along Hardy Canyon's green bottom, giving access to animal trails that climb the ridges. **Note:** Winter floods of 1995–96 undermined the bridge at the beginning of the Hardy Canyon road. The road may never be reopened.

Drive through Selah on South First Street. Turn right on Naches Avenue and go one long block before turning left on North Wenas Road. In a bit more than 18 miles (1.6 miles beyond Wenas Reservoir), turn left on the Hardy Canyon road. If the bridge has not been repaired, park here. In dry weather, and with care, the road can be driven about 1 mile, to an elevation of about 2400 feet. Here a choice must be made.

The decision may be made to park hereabouts and start walking; the road now enters Hardy Canyon, partly easy driving, partly mean and rocky, with few chances to turn around to beat a retreat. A wide spot at 0.9 mile from North Wenas Road is neatly convenient. As for the walking route—simply scramble up the hillside and ascend the ridge crest in flowers and views.

If the decision is made to wheel onward, follow the canyon road another 3 miles to about 3500 feet, where the way deteriorates to a 4WD track. Continue on foot to the 4924-foot east summit of Cleman Mountain.

Hardy Canyon Road

24 BLACK CANYON– UMTANUM RIDGE CREST

Length: round trip 4 to 6 miles
High point: 3900 feet (approximate)
Elevation gain: 1300 to 1500 feet (approximate)
Management: State Wildlife Department
USGS maps: Milk Creek, Hudson Creek, Wenas Lake

Subsequent to the last uplift of the Cascade Range a new rumpling of the earth's crust formed a system of ridges extending eastward from the Cascade Crest. These dry-side ridges never were sculptured by Pleistocene glaciers and thus retain gently rounded crests ideal for easy rambling. Umtanum Ridge is the quintessence and in these pages is the subject of a whole batch of splendid walks. The one described here is to the most westerly portion of the "desert-alpine" province, beyond which

Black Canyon

Umtanum Ridge

the elevations rise to snowier, thus wetter, thus more forested terrain. This stretch of the ridge has miles of dips and swells, summits and swales, where any vegetation taller than sagebrush is notable, where the steppe that in winter and summer seems a rocky barren comes vividly alive in May with vast splashes of buckwheat, poignant gardens of bitterroot. Though the ridge is traversed by a 4WD track beloved of the motorized Dan'l Boones, there's a plenty of lonesome space roamed mainly by deer, elk, and cows.

Two roads to the ridge crest are possibly negotiable by a family car. A nervy enough driver wealthy enough not to quail at the cost of paying a tow-truck fee can do much of the route on wheels. Feet are more dependable. Some stretches are easy pie and turnarounds are numerous if the going gets too rough. When one of the many steep and rocky stretches makes the family sedan scream for mercy, it's time to walk.

For the first road drive North Wenas Road some 18 miles from Selah and 0.1 mile past the Hardy Canyon road (see Hike 23) and turn right, uphill, on the Black Canyon road. (If the gate in the elk fence is closed, be certain to close it after passing through.) In 1.3 miles, at an elevation of about 2600 feet, decide whether to walk or ride.

Why fight it? From the decision point it's a mere 3 miles to the broad top of Umtanum Ridge, 3400 feet, and another 1 mile south on a 4WD track to a 3900-foot viewpoint south over the Wenas Valley and north to the Stuart Range. Just a nice morning's exercise, and never a worry about that tow truck.

For the second road drive North Wenas Road another 4 miles from the Black Canyon road, and at 0.3 mile short of the junction of the Audubon and Ellensburg roads, spot an unmarked dirt road climbing to the right. If the gate is closed, walk from here, elevation 2280 feet. If open, drive on—in most years the rough track can be endured by the family car. At 1 mile keep left. At about 1.3 miles is a second gate, beyond which the road usually dwindles to 4WD quality. Park here, elevation 2522 feet.

If the joy-boys are swarming, go elsewhere. However, many weekends of spring and nearly all weekdays the 4WD track is a peaceful walk, climbing in 2 miles from the second gate to the big-view, flower-bright crest of Umtanum Ridge, 3800 feet. If wheelers are too many, leave the 4WD track and strike off in any quiet direction, where you will.

25 AUDUBON CAMP

Length: round trip 1 to 4 miles
High point: 3198 or 3700 feet
Elevation gain: 1100 or 1300 feet
Management: Boise-Cascade
USGS map: Hudson Creek

Annually since 1963 the various Northwest groups of the Audubon Society have gathered Memorial Day weekend for a great big birding, botanizing, and socializing campout, the largest such gathering in the country. The base is Boise-Cascade's Audubon Camp. Partly because human interference in the natural scene is minimized, and largely because the location on the boundary of sagebrush-steppe and pine forest provides a wide variety of habitat, more than 200 species of birds have been identified—the largest known congregation of species in the state. Invitations to the campout are cordially extended to everyone, Audubon member or not. Just come. No knowledge is required, though it helps to be able to tell the difference between a robin and a dandelion. Audubon experts lead small groups in all directions to identify birds (the bluebirds are a particular favorite) and flowers. Needless to say, individuals can stage their own campouts any time they please.

To reach the Audubon Camp via the scenic and rude high route from Ellensburg, drive Umtanum Road up Shushuskin Canyon (see Hike 22), stay with Umtanum Road to Manastash Ridge, and finally descend to Wenas Valley. Some 13 miles of the road along the ridge are rough and dirty and sometimes mean.

For the recommended route on paved road, go off I-82 to Selah, drive through town on South First Street, turn right on Naches Avenue, and in one long block turn left on North Wenas Road. Proceed about 22.5 miles to a four-way junction at the end of pavement. Take the middle fork 3.2 miles, crossing North Fork Wenas Creek to the Audubon

Western bluebird's home in Audubon Campground

Wren's home near the Audubon Campground

Camp, elevation 2600 feet. The campground has no drinking water or picnic tables, but there are privies. Fortunately, the campground is huge for not only are there hundreds of Auduboners but dozens of horse camps and ORVers.

Three walking routes are suggested as introductions. The easiest is a rarely used logging road, barely passable to cars, that climbs from the northwest edge of the camp 2 miles to high views at Mud Flats, 3700 feet. At one spot or another a person likely will wish to leave the road and strike off cross-country.

For a more strenuous tour, from the south side of camp (opposite the entrance) cross open fields and Dry Creek (not dry in spring) and climb a cat track and then open slopes to a 3198-foot ridge crest overlooking farms of Wenas Valley.

For an all-day tour, cross North Fork Wenas Creek on the camp entry bridge. Ascend slopes to the east, sometimes following roads, sometimes just heading uphill. Patches of forest provide frequent cooling-off rest stops in the shade. The higher the way goes, the more the moisture from late melting of winter snows, and thus the more trees. From the ending point in a mosaic of pine groves and meadowy steppe at about 3900 feet on Manastash Ridge, the country eastward and downward is more open, and westward and upward more forested.

26 MANASTASH RIDGE

Length: round trip up to 4 miles
High point: 3930 feet
Elevation gain: 0 to 500 feet (approximate)
Management: State Wildlife Department
USGS map: Manastash Creek

Manastash Ridge is another of those wrinklings of the crust that reach east from the Cascades out into the Columbia River lava flows, another of those rounded highlands never plucked sharp and steep by ice, remaining mild and gentle for easy exploration. A network of rude

Mount Stuart from Manastash Ridge

Sunflowers

roads runs every which way, mostly barely passable, if at all, by a family car, but offering any number of good walking routes. No one destination stands out as better than others; everywhere are wide-open sagebrush-steppes and grassy meadows and tundra-like rock barrens colored by lupine, sunflowers, buckwheat, and bright pink bitterroot.

The best views and the best roaming are from the Wenas–Ellensburg road.

For the view, from the end of pavement on North Wenas Road (see Hike 25), drive 3.4 miles and turn left at a gate formerly signed "UW-OBS." (The sign was either missing in 1996 or lost amongst numerous driveways.) Within 1 mile of the gate the road crosses the first of several large meadows that cry out to be walked. At 5 miles the road reaches the dome-shaped University of Washington observatory, elevation 3930 feet. After the proper amount of gasping at spectacular views of the Stuart Range, walk the roads along the crest in both directions. Or, return to the large meadows and explore away from roads.

For miles of roaming drive on. At 7.4 miles from the pavement go left on an unsigned road 0.2 mile and park. For a 1½-mile flower walk climb the ridge to the right. The ridge top looks easy going but is actually very rough thanks to elk that have stomped deep pits when the ground was soft. Follow the crest past a grove of pine trees to a 4WD track near a pond, an easier return to the car. For a longer trip, leave the car when the going gets too tough and just keep the feet going and going and going.

27 WEST MANASTASH RIDGE

Length: round trip 2 to 11 miles
High point: 3300 feet
Elevation gain: 700 feet (approximate)
Management: State Wildlife Department
USGS maps: Hudson Creek, Manastash Creek

As is true of companion highlands, Manastash Ridge is not a single walking trip but many, countless. The stretch of crest on the west side of Manastash Creek offers miles of flowers on a broad, almost level sagebrush prairie.

Drive I-90 to Exit 109, go off right, and follow Canyon Road north 0.6 mile into Ellensburg. Turn left on Dammon Road 1.7 miles to a four-way intersection at a schoolhouse. The straight-ahead road changes name

North Fork Manastash Creek from West Manastash Ridge

here to Umtanum Road (see Hike 22). Turn right, west, on Manastash Road 10.8 miles to a narrow forest road and a stock-loading ramp. Known locally as Shell Rock Road, this unsigned track is too steep for the family car. Park, elevation 2600 feet.

Shell Rock Road ascends steeply in forest, flattens a bit, switchbacks right, and steepens again. In about $1/2$ mile the way emerges from trees and gets even steeper. In a scant 1 mile that gains 500 feet (very steep for a road and a pretty good tilt even for a trail), the track abruptly levels out. The next 4 miles alternate between meadow and forest. To escape the possibility of motor disturbance, at the top of the steep rise leave the road and ascend the knoll to the right, a 3258-foot overlook of the Manastash valley. Wander the ridge eastward from one little knoll to the next and walk every which way, though not all at the same time.

POTHOLES

Columbia National Wildlife Refuge

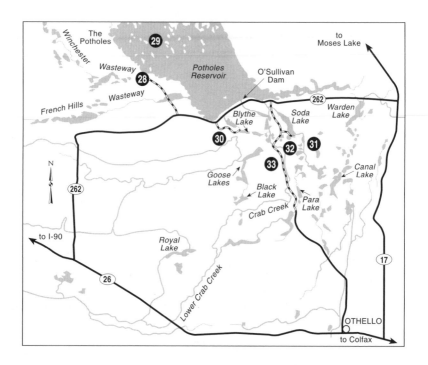

28 WINCHESTER WASTEWAY

Length: round trip 3 miles
High point: 1200 feet (approximate)
Elevation gain: 60 feet (approximate)
Management: State Wildlife Department
USGS map: Mae

Is it sagebrush that's wanted? There's no shortage hereabouts. Sand dunes also are in good supply—heaps of sterile mineral on the march, and heaps anchored by grasses. The light dressing of coarse black sand and the patches of white powder remind of Mount St. Helens, 1980. Complementing the enormous dryness are the little wetnesses of potholes ringed by reeds, nurturing distinctive plant communities. Things grow in the wet, inches from things that grow in the dry. Marshes and willow thickets enrich the scene on the up-and-down walk to the shore of Potholes Reservoir.

From O'Sullivan Road (see Hike 30) 3.4 miles west of Potholes State

Park, drive north on a gravel road signed "Public Fishing." In 1.2 miles cross Frenchman Hills Wasteway on a culvert. At 2 miles is an intersection. The left wanders out over the prairie to small ponds; keep straight ahead. From straight and wide, the road narrows, turns this way and that. At 2.2 miles turn right to the road-end, 3 miles from O'Sullivan Road. Elevation, 1040 feet.

Walk the concrete bridge over Winchester Wasteway and take the trail headed east. Paths branch off left and right; stick with the route that obviously is beaten by the most feet.

Winchester Wasteway

The trail ends in about 1½ miles atop a high sand dune overlooking the Winchester Wasteway entry into the reservoir. Gaze out upon the hundreds of tiny islands that before being surrounded by water were marching dunes like the one you're standing on.

29
POTHOLES ISLAND HIDEAWAY (OR DESERT ISLANDS)

Length: round trip 2 miles by boat
High point: 1040 feet
Elevation gain: none
Management: State Wildlife Department
USGS maps: Mae, Moses Lake South, O'Sullivan Dam

Mountains of sand to roll around in. Sandy beaches for swimming and sunbathing. Desert islands, hideaways, private retreats that can only be reached by boat. Since some of the water is only inches deep, a canoe is best.

Potholes Reservoir

Air view of Potholes Reservoir

When the irrigation water was turned on in the 1940s, the Potholes Reservoir behind O'Sullivan Dam flooded miles of active sand dunes south of Moses Lake. Many were drowned but the higher ones became islands. Over the past half-century the wind has pushed much of the sand into the water and due to the flooding has not been able to replenish the supply. However, enough islands still remain to fill days of explorations.

Drive O'Sullivan Road (see Hike 30) to the boat-launching area of Potholes State Park. Elevation, 1040 feet. The wind can sometimes be mean. If so, canoeists may want to embark at the more protected North Potholes area.

Once on the water, pick your island, but watch where you are; it's easy to get lost in the maze of waterways. Water, water everywhere, but not a drop to drink. As the season goes along, the lake turns a pretty shade of green. Bring your own liquids.

30 BLYTHE LAKE AND COULEE

Length: round trip 1 to 5 miles
High point: 1248 feet
Elevation gain: 200 to 350 feet (approximate)
Management: Columbia National Wildlife Area
USGS map: O'Sullivan Dam

Cliffs above Blythe Lake

High buttes give long views over the sagebrush-steppe. Cliffs portray the history of millions of years of lava flows. Basalt columns have an eerie resemblance to ruins of some ancient civilization. Lakes reflect the blue of the big sky and catch the winds of spring, rippling and sparkling. Everywhere are animal tracks to follow, puzzling out the destinations of the residents of the Columbia National Wildlife Area.

From I-90, on the east side of Vantage Bridge, go right and follow SR 26 about 20 miles. Turn left on a county road signed "Ephrata" and "Potholes State Park" for 5 miles, then go right onto O'Sullivan Road to a point 500 feet west of Mar Don Resort

Moon setting above Blythe Lake

and near a maintenance shop and storage area. Turn south 1.7 miles to the Blythe Lake parking area, elevation 900 feet.

Walk the gated road to the end and climb a well-defined trail several hundred feet to a bluff overlooking Blythe Lake. Pause to choose the day's destination.

One option is to follow the bluff to more views of Blythe Lake, Chukar Lake, and marshes of Crab Creek. Eventually the trail connects to a gravel road (gated) from the south.

Another is to explore inland, down in the canyons, up on the rolling hills. Explore wherever and as far as suits the fancy, from one canyon and hill to the next. The highest point is 1248 feet. Keep close note of where you're wandering—though the route never is more than a mile or two from the start, circling around can make a long day.

31 POTHOLES CANAL

Length: round trip 1 to 5 miles
High point: 1000 feet
Elevation gain: on return 100 feet (approximate)
Management: Columbia National Wildlife Area
USGS map: Soda Lake

Dwarf waterleaf

A service road (gated against wheels), open to hiking from March 1 through July 31, follows the banks of Potholes Canal, threading through canyons to views over dozens of lakes and potholes.

From I-90 on the east side of Vantage Bridge, go right and follow SR 26 about 20 miles. Turn left on a county road signed "Ephrata" and "Potholes State Park" for 5 miles, then go right onto O'Sullivan Road along the meandering crest of earthen O'Sullivan Dam, which forms Potholes Reservoir. At the east end of the dam turn south and drive 2.4 miles into Columbia National Wildlife Area. Go left 0.6 mile on the Pillar and Widgeon Lakes road to a large parking area, elevation 1000 feet.

Bittern

Walk the road past the gate. Keep left at the first Y and left again at the second. In about ¹/₂ mile cross the dam forming Elbow Lake to the Potholes Canal service road. Proceed south, passing close above Pillar, Snip, Cattail, and Sago Lakes, in view of many other seepages from the reservoir. At about 2¹/₂ miles the route leaves the canal and drops to Hampton Lake, 901 feet.

32   CRAB CREEK TRAILS

Management: Columbia National Wildlife Area
USGS map: Soda Lake

The Columbia National Wildlife Area and the state's Seeps Lakes Wildlife Recreation Area have some of the most interesting sagebrush-steppe trails in this book. Although the drive-to lakes in the two areas are visited by thousands, the three trails along Crab Creek are so seldom used they are almost lost.

Crab Creek

Frog Lake trail

Crab Creek Trail

Length: round trip 1 mile
Elevation gain: none

Few feet walk this ¹/₂-mile interpretive trail in the riparian zone along Crab Creek. A pity.

From the east end of O'Sullivan Dam drive south on a gravel road into Columbia National Wildlife Area (see Hike 31). At the Pillar–Widgeon Lakes road junction, go right another 0.8 mile to the large Crab Creek trailhead parking area on the south side of the road.

Hike across a meadow to a large interpretive sign. From there the trail crosses Crab Creek on a bridge and climbs a few steps.

Frog Lake Trail

Length: round trip 2 miles
High point: 960 feet
Elevation gain: 60 feet (approximate)

In the topsy-turvy lava scabland, the wetland reeds and grasses and sedges and shrubs contrast pleasantly with the enormous drylands of sagebrush all around. This vicinity has so many lakes that even the

Crab Creek tributary

USGS map gives up on trying to name them all. The Frog Lake trail described here is open for hiking from March 1 to July 31.

From the Crab Creek trailhead go left on Othello Road 1 mile to a parking area on the right, elevation 900 feet.

Walk across the road and down to the broad, graveled, earth dam impounding Crab Creek. From the far side of the dam go left, upstream, to the end of gravel and the start of true trail. With a few steep exceptions, the way climbs gently 1 mile to Frog Lake, 960 feet.

The trail continues to a high point 1¼ miles from the road. Here is a three-way split. Try any or all of the three. Each explores the contorted scabland and its potholes, basalt pinnacles, and the cliffs that may once have been the site of a mighty waterfall. For views of Gadwall Lake, take the right-hand trail to the top of the ridge.

Marsh Loop Trail

Length: round trip 1¾ miles

Starting from the Frog Lake trail, this path is differentiated by circling a marsh to which thirsty birds flock in crowds.

Drive to the Frog Lake trailhead, cross Crab Creek on the footbridge, and find the Marsh Loop trail headed south.

33 GOOSE LAKES PLATEAU

Length: round trip 3 to 5 miles
High point: 1050 feet (approximate)
Elevation gain: 200 feet (approximate)
Management: Columbia National Wildlife Area and State Wildlife Department
USGS maps: O'Sullivan Dam, Soda Lake

Two chapters in the history of the Seeps Lakes Wildlife Recreation Area give it special interest. An ancient chapter features glaciers—that is, melted glaciers. Some 20,000 years ago an ice dam (repeatedly) broke in Montana and the enormous Lake Missoula (repeatedly) emptied out over the Columbia Plateau, scouring the Channeled Scablands

Goose Lakes Plateau

whose canyons and cliffs are at their most spectacular here. A recent chapter features fire—flames that raced and roared across the prairies in 1984, burning the sagebrush, to be replaced (temporarily) by a vastness of grass, rich green in spring. The 4 square miles of the WRA are the most various and exciting in the Potholes area for scenery and flowers.

Of the two ways to the Goose Lakes Plateau, the quickest is from the road-end at Upper Goose Lake, elevation 861 feet. A onetime 4WD road, closed to vehicles, leads ½ mile to grasslands of the burn.

The longer and prettier way is up a photogenic coulee, starting from the Morgan Lakes road. From the east end of O'Sullivan Dam, drive south into Columbia National Wildlife Area (see Hike 31). Go south 3.2 miles to a split. Straight ahead is Upper Goose Lake and the quick route. Left 1 mile on the Morgan Lakes road is the Frog Lake trailhead. Because it is impossible to get the car off the road at the start of the plateau trail, park here and walk ⅖ mile to the trailhead, elevation 850 feet.

From the looks of the tread the trail was once popular but now is seldom used—apparently because of the loss of parking; the addition of ⅖ mile with a cloud of dust from every passing car has discouraged pedestrians. A gate intended to exclude vehicles (here officially banned) is rusted shut; take the easy bypass to the right. Beyond the fence the trail climbs 200 feet and enters a wide coulee walled on either side by basalt cliffs 200 feet high. In ¾ mile the coulee bends left and in another ½ mile right, intersecting an abandoned 4WD track. Two choices: Follow the track left, up to the plateau, or stay in the coulee another ½ mile to the plateau. Roam on, roam on, over the plateau towards Lower Goose Lake.

WENATCHEE AREA

Colockum Wildlife Recreation Area

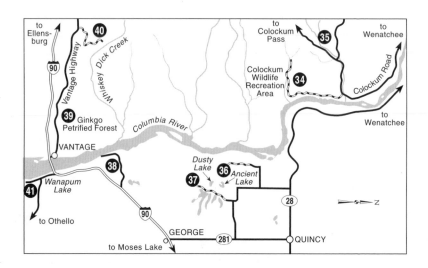

34 COLOCKUM WILDLIFE RECREATION AREA

Length: round trip short hike 3 miles; long hike 8 miles
High point: short hike 1958 feet; long hike 3200 feet
Elevation gain: short hike 820 feet; long hike 2100 feet
Management: State Wildlife Department
USGS maps: Malago, Stay Gulch, West Bar

The Colockum Wildlife Recreation Area and adjacent Quilomene Wildlife Recreation Area form the largest expanse of Washington "desert" in state ownership. Rising from the Columbia River to the heights of Mission Ridge, the varied ecosystems abound in wildlife in winter, flowers in spring. For the flowers, no one time is perfect for the whole area. At any spot the bloom lasts only a few weeks, but the color show begins early near the river and climbs through the months, following the edge of the melting snow. First are yellow bells, grass widows, and shooting stars. Later there are the golden yellow of sunflowers (a designation applied to many species, including balsamroot), the white and pink and violet of phlox, the blue of lupine and larkspur.

Warning: Roads of the WRA are dirt—dusty in dry weather, axle-deep mud in wet. In any season they are barely passable in a family car.

In Wenatchee, stay on the west side of the Columbia River and go downstream on Wenatchee Avenue. At the East Wenatchee Bridge underpass follow the road signed "Malaga." Wenatchee Avenue becomes South Wenatchee Avenue, then Malaga-Alcoa, and finally Colockum

Road. From the underpass drive almost 14 miles, passing Malaga and Rock Island Dam, to an intersection. Go left on Tarpiscan Road. In 1.6 miles enter the Colockum WRA, and at 3.1 miles come to a junction near a large tank. The right fork goes to the headquarters building; go left (straight ahead) on a rough dirt road. Everywhere are hiking possibilities. The hills are inviting. So are the little beaches along the river, nestled between cliffs. For openers, drive the dirt road 2 miles, passing Davis Canyon, to a large parking area, elevation 1130 feet.

A short hike and a long hike can be made from here. For both, at the far end of the parking area, near a creek, find a well-defined trail that climbs a bit above the brushy creekbed. In a long ¼ mile the valley branches.

For the short hike, go straight ahead to an abandoned truck track that makes one long switchback and ends halfway up the hill. The way is open and obvious to the summit, 1958 feet, 1½ miles from the car. Views are magnificent over the valley of Tarpiscan Creek and the Columbia River to wheatfields and the infinite-seeming ridges of the WRA.

For the long hike, where the valley branches go right, climb the open hillside, on animal paths as much as possible. Continue to the first high point, then the next, and the next, to steadily broader views across the river to farms, cattle, and Moses Coulee. Tiny flowers and

Elk, Colockum Wildlife Recreation Area

miniature sagebrush grow on the high rocks. The ridge keeps climbing to timberline but a good turnaround is a 3200-foot high point about 4 miles from the car, just short of powerlines.

35 COLOCKUM PASS ROAD

Length: round trip ½ to 5 miles
High point: 2500 feet (approximate)
Elevation gain: 200 to 400 feet (approximate)
Management: State Wildlife Department
USGS map: Malaga

The historically interesting stagecoach road from Ellensburg to Wenatchee, crossing 6371-foot Colockum Pass, is impossible most of the year for the family car. Indeed, most of the primitive roads in the transition zone between farmland and forest are tough wheeling. The

Colockum Wildlife Recreation Area

big advantage this trip has over others in the Colockum Wildlife Recreation Area is that the hiking can start a short way from paved road. The great attraction is the good walking on ridges rich in the spring with flowers that down by the Columbia River have already passed their bloom.

From Wenatchee drive downstream on the southwest side of the Columbia River 14 miles on the road signed "Malaga" (see Hike 34). At the Tarpiscan Road junction stay on Colockum Road. At 4.8 miles, at a sharp turn go straight, entering the Colockum WRA in 0.8 mile. Just short of the corrals and barns go right on a one-lane road as far as the family car permits. Get out and walk, elevation 2200 feet.

From wherever, hike wherever you please, as far as you please, until you've had your day's fill of flowers. Animal paths will take you to whatever destination you choose.

36 ANCIENT LAKES

Length: round trip 8 miles
High point: 1100 feet (approximate)
Elevation gain: 100 feet (approximate)
Management: State Wildlife Department
USGS map: Babcock Ridge

Three lakes in a wide coulee offer flowers (in early spring, acres of yellow bells) and scenery (columnar basalt) and, in addition, a good chance of solitude, because 24 other lakes in the Quincy Wildlife Recreation Area are quicker to get to. Easy enough a day hike though the route is, the neat notion is to backpack. Carry a stove; there's no forest. Lie out on the lone prairie where the stars at night are big and bright. Join the coyotes in serenading the moon.

Two routes lead to these remote lakes, a lower, nearly level way in a wide coulee and a higher, longer way past small lakes, a waterfall, and a short scramble under columnar basalt cliffs.

Lower Route

From the center of Quincy drive west 4 miles on SR 28 and between mileposts 25 and 26 turn south on U NW, signed "White Trail Road." In 1 mile from the highway turn right on 9 NW. Pavement ends at 2.9 miles from U NW; at 5.9 miles the road turns right to the last farmhouse. Go straight ahead a few more feet to a small parking space and the entry to the WRA and a gate, elevation 1000 feet.

Walk the minor ups and downs of the gated 4WD track ½ mile to a junction. The straight-ahead fork leads 3 miles to Dusty Lake (Hike 37). The left goes 3½ miles in Potholes Coulee to its abrupt end in a

Upper Route to Ancient Lakes

rimrock cliff and the three Ancient Lakes—remnants of the true and
much larger Ancient Lake, which filled much of the coulee until it
(probably) found an underground outlet through lava tubes. Two of the
lakes are side by side. Find the third a bit farther, hidden by a small
ridge.

Upper Route

Stay on U NW, which at a bend becomes 5 NW. At 5.9 miles from SR
28 turn right on a dirt road marked with fishing and hunting signs. At
0.5 mile enter the WRA and at 0.8 mile from the pavement find a large
parking area near a cottonwood grove and a gated service road.

Walk the road about ⅓ mile to a power tower. Take the left branch
and watch for a cave on the right that looks like an old fumarole. The
road becomes a footpath descending to a small lake on the edge of a

cliff. At the lake the cliff looks like a long dive, but a trail finds its way under some columnar basalt to a scree slope. Extreme care is needed for a short but steep descent with a great view of the lake's outlet pouring over the cliff.

Below the cliff the trail crosses a stream, comes to a view of Ancient Lakes, and proceeds down to the lakes' valley.

37 DUSTY LAKE

Length: round trip 3 miles
High point: 1200 feet
Elevation gain: on return 368 feet
Management: State Wildlife Department
USGS map: Babcock Ridge

A trail! An honest-to-gosh trail! And more's the wonder, in the Quincy Wildlife Recreation Area! Delights for all the senses: sight (reddish basalt cliffs spattered with yellow and red lichens); sound

One of the small lakes on the Dusty Lake trail

(waterfalls, birds that live at five small lakes along the way); smell (flowers and sage); feel (the fresh air of springtime breezes); and taste (lunch).

From the center of Quincy drive west 4 miles on SR 28 and between mileposts 25 and 26 turn south on U NW, signed "White Trail Road." At a turn the road becomes 5 NW. At 5.9 miles from the highway go right on a gravel road with a state sign advertising hunting and fishing. (Alternately, approach from SR 281.) In 0.5 mile enter the WRA. Drive 2.1 miles more, passing three large lakes, to the Dusty Lake trailhead parking lot, elevation 1200 feet.

The trail drops to a creek crossing and climbs a few feet to the brink of a cliff, descends a diagonal ledge, and levels out. The way crosses a second stream to the brink of a second cliff and descends via a break in an otherwise very formidable wall. At 1½ miles is Dusty Lake, 832 feet. (A puzzle: Having crossed the two inlet streams on the way, one wonders where the water goes—the lake has no outlet. Into the underground lava tubes, no doubt.)

Between the two cliffs are numerous footpaths to the five little lakes, home to redwing blackbirds, yellow-headed blackbirds, and lots of waterfowl.

Dusty Lake also can be reached from the abandoned Ancient Lakes 4WD track (see Hike 36) but shore cliffs rule out a walk around the lake for a one-way trip.

38 FRENCHMAN COULEE

Length: round trip 2 to 3 miles
High point: 800 feet (approximate)
Elevation gain: 200 feet (approximate)
Management: State Wildlife Department
USGS map: Evergreen Ridge

The Quincy Wildlife Recreation Area features vast sweeps of sagebrush-steppe, of course, and millions of bright flowers in season, also of course. In addition there are a few sand dunes and, most spectacularly, some of the region's finest basalt "picket fences." Frenchman Coulee is within a separate segment of the WRA on an abandoned section of old US 10, which once led to a ferry crossing of the Columbia River near Vantage.

The good news is that the ORVs which once tracked this are now almost entirely gone. The bad news is that fencing off the wheels also made life a little more difficult for feet.

From I-90 between Vantage and George, drive to Exit 143, signed "Silica Road," as well as "George Amphitheater—Wanapum Lake" (reservoir). Drive this road 0.7 mile and go left (unsigned in 1996) on old US 10; contrast this narrow and twisty highway, built for Model Ts, with I-90. Progress! The road winds down cliffs, in spectacular views of Frenchman Coulee, crosses the wide Babcock Bench, and in 5.3 miles reaches the banks of the reservoirized Columbia River near the former site of the Vantage Ferry, the crossing now drowned (as is the river) by the reservoir of Wanapum Dam. Progress! Park at the road-end, elevation 570 feet.

There are three starting points for hikers. For a short walk follow US 10 for 2.2 miles from the Silica Road, to a pullout below a picket fence of giant columnar basalt.

For longer hikes go 0.3 mile farther and find a parking lot where a closed 4WD track takes off, climbing into an unnamed coulee with trails and 4WD tracks this way and that. If lucky find a nice-sized lake.

For wandering, drive the final 3 miles to the edge of Wanapum Reservoir and a huge parking lot. The fence has two people-only openings.

Basalt columns at Frenchman Coulee

The one near the boat launch is probably the best. Intersect the gated service road and walk downstream until stopped by cliffs. Climb 200 feet on another 4WD track to Babcock Bench and walk back to some small sand dunes.

39 TREES OF STONE

Length: round trip ³/₄ mile
High point: 1300 feet (approximate)
Elevation gain: 250 feet (approximate)
Management: Ginkgo Petrified Forest State Park
USGS map: Ginkgo

How does a forest trail qualify as a desert hike? Easy—when there's no shade. The Douglas fir, redwood, spruce, maple, elm, and ginkgo (the sacred tree of Chinese temples) that once flourished here fell down 15 million years ago. They fell into a lake and thus didn't burn when hot lava flowed over them. Buried deep under basalt, the cellulose of the trees was replaced, cell by cell, by silica. Ice Age floods and subsequent erosion have uncovered hundreds of petrified trees in the Vantage area. However, only those in the 7635-acre Ginkgo Petrified Forest State Park are truly protected from mining and exploitation.

For centuries Indians camped along the Columbia near Vantage. On a wall of columnar basalt behind their camp, they carved petroglyphs, one of the best examples of their art in the Northwest. In the early 1930s Dr. George Beck, scientist, poet, geologist, and professor at Ellensburg Normal School, helped persuade the state legislature to protect the area as Gingko State Park. During the Great Depression, the WPA (Works Progress Administration) built a museum on a cliff overlooking the Columbia River, a riverside trail to the petroglyphs, and an interpretive trail 2 miles inland to "The Trees of Stone," twenty-one petrified trees. In 1937 I followed Dr. Beck as he led our class on the "Trees of Stone" trail, then overland miles to look at trees that were above-ground. Next we took the riverside trail to the petroglyphs where he explained how they were made and speculated what the symbols meant. While it took 15 million years to create a forest of stone and centuries for the petroglyphs to be carved; it has taken one lifetime for vandals to force the park to fence off the above-ground petrified trees and for a power-hungry nation to destroy the Indian art (a crude attempt was made to move the petroglyphs to the museum).

Drive I-90 to Exit 136 at Vantage, turn north to the museum to see what remains of the petroglyphs, and go 2 miles more to the self-guiding ³/₄-mile Trees of Stone nature trail. For views and flowers, a longer trail leaves the nature trail at an elevation of 1050 feet. For lack of personnel, entry to the rest of the state park, with logs lying above the ground, is restricted.

Indian pictographs in Gingko Petrified Forest State Park which were destroyed by the rising water behind Wanapum Dam.

40 WHISKEY DICK MOUNTAIN

Length: round trip 1 to 10 miles
High point: 3000 feet or so
Elevation gain: 300 to 800 feet
Management: State Wildlife Department
USGS maps: Whiskey Dick Mtn., Boylston

The view from Whiskey Dick Mountain covers 200 square miles—
and not a tree in sight. But there are, to the west, Mount Rainier, the
Goat Rocks, and Mount Adams and, to the east, the Columbia River,
irrigated farmland towards Moses Lake, and miles of sagebrush hills
rolling like dry waves in a desert landscape.

The highest summit, 3873 feet, appears to be on private land with
no public access and lies at the west end of the 14-mile mountain ridge
undulating easterly, at last descending to the Columbia River at 738
feet. A 3003-foot lesser summit thicketed by communication towers can
be seen directly north of the Vantage Highway summit pass, reached
by a road signed "No Trespassing." Any of the many lesser summits

Hedgehog cactus

has the big views and in season flowers are everywhere, high and low. The bitterroot and hedgehog cactus of rocky slopes are not rare but neither are they everyday excitements in a wildland-walker's life.

The two suggested accesses to Whiskey Dick Mountain run through the Quilomene Wildlife Recreation Area. For the first, drive the Vantage Highway (formerly old US 10) between Ellensburg and Vantage to milepost 19 (missing in 1996) or 5.6 miles west from the Ginkgo Trees of Stone trailhead (see Hike 39) and enter the Quilomene WRA. The second access is 1.8 miles farther or, driving from Ellensburg, 1.8 miles from the summit. Both accesses are on the north side of the road and easy to miss. The WRA roads deteriorate to 4WD condition that may be too rough for a family car; when the going gets tough, the smart get walking.

For the first access, the family car may with a groan be able to drive the 0.4 mile to a junction. If flowers are the main interest park here and wander afoot east and west. If peakbagging is the challenge, drive or walk another mile northward and park on the edge of Rock Coulee, at the next junction, 2300 feet.

Walk the narrow rough road downhill, losing 150 feet, then climb steeply towards the highest bump on the ridge, gaining a good 1100 feet. Small chips of petrified wood in the roadway testify to illegal mining by vandals.

The road for the second access (from Vantage) is so rough the family car definitely will beg to be parked near the highway, elevation 2300 feet.

The road inveigles the optimist by being good the first few hundred feet and then, past a spring, throws off the smiling mask to reveal a grim, steep 4WD visage. In about 1/3 mile is a 2600-foot summit. If flowers are the purpose of the trip, walk eastward. If sweeping views are the goal, continue on the 4WD track, losing some 200 feet on an easy descent into Rock Coulee, then climbing to one of Whiskey Dick's summits, your choice.

41 WANAPUM BREAKS

Length: round trip 1 to 5 miles
High point: 1100 feet (approximate)
Elevation gain: 100 to 600 feet
Management: nobody in sight
USGS map: Vantage

As the mountains rose up, the Columbia River kept cutting down, maintaining its course. Wanapum Breaks, the steep hillside above Wanapum Dam, has some of the best and earliest wildflowers. There are, as well, wind-rippled sand dunes, walls of columnar basalt, and long views of sagebrush hills above the reservoirized river. Lack of

Wanapum Breaks

fences and signs encourage exploring—that's the good news. The bad news is that if hikers feel invited, so do ORVers, taking particular delight in rampaging through fragile terrain. Though not posted, these slopes may be on private land, and if so the wheels are sure to ultimately cause "No Trespassing" signs.

There are five possible accesses. For the first drive I-90 to the east end of Vantage Bridge, turn south a scant mile, and park near the junction of road Nos. 26 and 243. The second access is 1.7 miles farther on road No. 243. A third (best from a hiker's standpoint) is at 2.2 miles, the fourth is about 3.5 miles, at the abandoned Wanapum Dam Viewpoint above the dam, and the fifth is another 5 miles, at the crossing of Lower Crab Creek, near a large sand dune.

From whichever access, walk uphill, along the way exploring side gullies to the powerlines on the crest. The largest sand dunes are east of the powerlines. ORV tracks are disgustingly numerous but much of the terrain is too difficult for wheels, though easy enough for feet. Explore the scabland of shattered rocks and basalt cliffs, the sand dunes, the little rock gardens. Wander uphill to the power towers and wide views this way and that along the Columbia's trench through the mountains.

42 EAST SADDLE MOUNTAIN

Length: round trip 1 mile
High point: 2067 feet
Elevation gain: 300 feet going; on return 150 feet (approximate)
Management: State Wildlife Department
USGS map: Corfu

The Saddle Mountains are 50 miles long, on both sides of the Columbia River, which slices through the range at Wahluke Gap, the river's downcutting having kept pace with the ridge's uprising. High in the wind at the east end, views from the flower gardens extend north to the quiltwork of farms and the meanders of Crab Creek, south to the Columbia River, and west to Mount Rainier and the tip of Mount Adams.

Drive SR 24 west from Mattawa or east from Othello. Between mileposts 60 and 61 turn north on a narrow, paved road aimed straight at the mountains. The road tilts, climbing to a ridgetop split. The left fork

Saddle Mountain

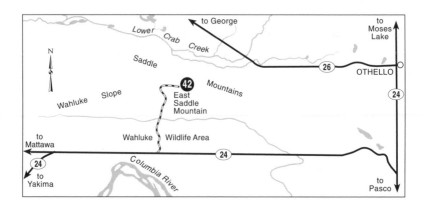

is a graveled road along the crest. Take the right, paved, to an abandoned military installation at the road-end, 5.4 miles from the highway. Park here, elevation 1980 feet.

Walk the crest, through a miniaturized desert garden where the sagebrush is only 6 inches tall and the clusters of phlox blossoms are tiny to match. In all seasons the lichen on the rocks is colorful. The crest is broken by a deep saddle; stay to the right of cliffs, drop 150 feet, then climb steeply to the rounded summit of shattered rock, 2067 feet, 1/2 mile from the car.

Not that the views get any bigger, but the wide, gently rolling ridge can be walked another 1 1/2 miles with a loss of only 200 feet before the crest drops away and down. More flowers. More lichen. More good springtime winds.

LOWER GRAND COULEE

Bitterroot

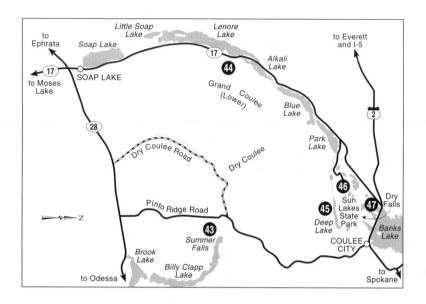

43   SUMMER FALLS

Length: round trip 2 to 5 miles
High point: 1640 feet
Elevation gain: 300 feet
Management: Sun Lakes State Park
USGS maps: Coulee City, Stratford, Wilson Creek NW

The falls had no name, of course, when meltwater from the continental ice sheet was pouring over the basalt cliffs. Afterward, for thousands of years, the falls didn't exist, and they weren't reborn until the Columbia Basin Reclamation Project exploited the ancient channels for reservoirs and spillways. The name was given because for a time the water definitely did fall in summer, when spigots of the storage reservoirs were opened to feed irrigation canals. But then a power plant was built, diverting most of the flow through turbines, and Summer Falls became a mere summer dribble into Billy Clapp Reservoir. Other than that, however, the coulee and cliff scenery is as dramatic as ever in the Stratford and Long Lake Wildlife Recreation Areas. Additionally, green slopes by the lake (reservoir) are covered with shooting star in April; later, the rock rim above has a delightful showing of bright pink bitterroot blossoms.

From SR 28 east of Soap Lake, between mileposts 61 and 62, drive north 6.3 miles on Pinto Ridge Road, following signs for Summer Falls

State Park. Proceed to the lowest point of the enormous parking lot, elevation 1340 feet. (The park also can be reached by Dry Coulee Road, dusty but very scenic.)

Walk a lakeshore trail about ¼ mile past an old fence line and climb the steep green slopes to the ridge top, 1640 feet. The view is grand down to the reservoir, Summer Falls, and the powerhouse, though when the *Lewisia rediviva* is in climax underfoot the eyes scarcely can focus on the distance.

Walk east along the rocky rim another long mile, detouring around the heads of gullies, passing beneath two powerlines, the views and flowers continuous. A steep descent returns to the lakeshore.

Summer Falls as it is now and Billy Clapp Reservoir

44 THE GRAND COULEE— LENORE LAKE CAVE SHELTERS

Length: round trip ½ mile
High point: 1100 feet (approximate)
Elevation gain: 50 feet (approximate)
Management: State Wildlife Department
USGS maps: Little Soap Lake, Park Lake

What Mount Rainier is to the High Cascades, the Grand Coulee is to the Columbia Plateau. Having served Nature's purpose as channel for waters from the continental ice sheet, for thousands of years the great gash was left to itself, lonesome dryland. Then the engineers gave it a new purpose, part of the water-distribution system of the Columbia Basin Reclamation Project. Lakes were formed. Fish planted. Tourists thronged, most with one-track minds. Make that two-track. Admire the pretty lakes. Catch those fish. Pleasant diversions, to be sure. However, there are pretty lakes and fat fish elsewhere. For a hiker the highest and best use of this place is to explore the towering walls of

Lenore Lake Cave Shelter

Grand Coulee

lava flows, layer piled atop layer, the somber hues of the rock contrasting with the yellow and orange lichen, with the springtime rainbow of flowers in bloom.

SR 17 and SR 155 traverse the entire 47 miles of Grand Coulee from Soap Lake to Grand Coulee Dam. At the legal speed limit of 65 miles per hour, the scenery and flowers flash by in 45 minutes, permitting the traveler to collect his decal and speed on for an hour at Mount Rainier and a quick spin around Crater Lake. Such folks as this never see Grand Coulee; the sharpest memories they will carry home are of the 47-mile highway gridlock and perhaps the traffic accidents. To see the Grand, a visitor must slow down to 2 miles per hour, maximum, and that is best done without wheels, afoot.

Trips in this book describe many ways to explore the Grand Coulee and companion coulees which are nearly as grand. However, a major attraction of the area—the flowers—is nowhere better than beside the highway. Whatever else a visitor does or doesn't, he should get out and walk a few hundred feet (or a few miles). No single destination can be nominated as best—there are 47 glorious flower miles. The thing to do is drive along with an eye out for (1) splashes of color and (2) a turnout where the car can be parked without aggravating the gridlock and triggering collisions of vehicles hurrying from fishing hole to fishing hole. For a starter, try the area between mileposts 81 and 82, beside Lenore

Lake, where several fishing-access spots on the lake side of the highway are convenient for parking, elevation 1100 feet.

A special feature, not to be missed, is the cave shelters beside Lenore Lake. The monster floods that dug the Grand Coulee scoured away lenses of weaker rock between layers of hard basalt, forming caves. Families of nomads traveling through to hunt and gather found good camping in them. From SR 17 near the upper end of Lenore Lake a well-signed gravel road leads to the trailhead, elevation 1150 feet. The four caves are about ¼ mile from the cars on a surfaced path; the one steep section is a cement stairway.

Two larger caves above Park Lake are on private land. State Park officials are negotiating to obtain public access.

45 COULEE CITY STAGECOACH ROAD— DEEP LAKE

Length: round trip to viewpoint 2 miles; to lakeshore 1½ miles
High point: viewpoint 1550 feet; lakeshore 1400 feet (approximate)
Elevation gain: to viewpoint 300 feet; to lakeshore 150 feet (approximate)
Management: Sun Lakes State Park
USGS map: Coulee City

History: the route of the Ephrata-to-Coulee City Stagecoach Road, climbing steeply from the Grand Coulee to the canyon brink. Scenery: from the brink, views down to 1½-mile-long Deep Lake, which has the look of a Norway fjord magically transported to the desert. From the lakeshore, views over the waters to the cliffs.

At Sun Lakes State Park, between the campground and day-use area, find the Deep Lake road. At a junction, keep right. At 2.1 miles park at the start of a dirt service road, elevation 1250 feet.

Walk the service road, which soon deteriorates to a 4WD track, the bed of the old stagecoach road. In about ⅓ mile the way turns up a side canyon and climbs steeply. Near the top a fence marks the boundary between public land and the King Ranch. The rancher has kindly provided an easy-open gate for hikers, so unless there is a change of heart and a "No Trespassing" sign, proceed to the top of the rise, 1550 feet, and peer over the brink, down the cliffs, a vertical 300 feet to Deep Lake.

But the day is not yet done. Return to the car and drive to the road-end campground at Deep Lake.

Walk the trail along the right-hand shoreline. In ½ mile the shoreline becomes cliffy; climb over the top and continue ¼ mile for more views and flowers before more cliffs call a halt.

Stagecoach road climbing out of the Grand Coulee

46 MONUMENT COULEE

Length: round trip 3 miles
High point: 1300 feet (approximate)
Elevation gain: 100 feet (approximate)
Management: Sun Lakes State Park
USGS map: Coulee City

Monument Valley, on the Navaho Indian Nation, is world famous for rock towers sculpted by wind erosion into shapes eerily resembling the graveyard of a race of titans. Sun Lakes State Park has turrets and cliffs also monumental, if not as awesomely as those in the valley. Still,

Monument Coulee

they are striking enough, evidencing the erosive power of the gigantic floods in Ice Age time. The scenery compensates for the relative paucity of flowers.

The easiest trail, preferred by horses, traverses the right side of the coulee. The most scenic way, more a route than a trail, is on the left. Scenery is what this hike is about; a person who comes solely for the two little lakes does better to take the short trail from Dry Falls Lake.

In Sun Lakes State Park, drive the Deep Lake–Dry Falls Lake road 1 mile and turn left on the paved road signed "Camp Delany." In 0.15 mile from the junction cross the unmarked horse trail. At 0.4 mile turn right at the sign "Camp Delany" and park near the camp gate, elevation 1200 feet.

Walk through the gate and go left 150 feet to find the abandoned 4WD track up the coulee. To the left are 300-foot cliffs of Umatilla Rock, once an island in the middle of Dry Falls. Ahead are strange towers leaning at odd angles. Follow the 4WD track as far as possible, passing near Camp Delany and Delany Springs, then select one of the many animal traces ascending the coulee. Often every sort of path fades away in grassy opens; no matter, the way is obvious, the only care required being to dodge around the potholes that dot the coulee floor.

In about 1¼ miles, at the north end of Umatilla Rock, go off left a few feet for a view of Dry Falls Lake. Look across the lake to the Dry Falls Interpretive Center, atop the cliff. Now go right, dropping 100 feet in ¼ mile to Red Alkali Lake, ringed by cattails; a stone's throw away is Green Lake, ringed by grass. Elevation, 1200 feet.

47 DRY FALLS CAVE

Length: round trip 1 mile
High point: 1581 feet
Elevation gain: on return 400 feet
Management: Sun Lakes State Park
USGS maps: Coulee City, Park Lake

The falls certainly weren't dry in Pleistocene times, when the floodwaters from Montana periodically roared across the Columbia Plateau. The waterfall of that era, 400 feet high and 3 miles wide, would make Niagara look like a leaky faucet. Displays at the Interpretive Center prepare for the descent to the bottom of Dry Falls, during which the imagination can replay in the mind those dramatic days of the Really Old West. The lake in the floor of the Grand Coulee and the cave at the base of the falls are added fillips.

Drive SR 17 to Dry Falls Overlook and Interpretive Center. Find the unmarked trail at the north end of the parking area, elevation 1581 feet.

Air view of Dry Falls cave located under the cliff

The trail starts by descending a concrete stairway equipped with a thank-golly steel handrail, contours an airy ledge some 3 to 4 feet (not enough) wide to another concrete stairway, followed by a steel stairway, another airy-scary ledge, and finally a for-real trail down a steep rockslide to the lakeshore. A flat path leads several hundred feet to the cave, elevation 1207 feet.

Note those elevations: The trip starts by losing 400 feet, easy enough for anyone except an acrophobe. It concludes by gaining 400 feet, which can be mighty warm for those mad dogs and Englishmen who go out in the midday sun.

Flowers are few on the trail. However, the cliff swallows are abundant and in nesting season take unkindly to intruders. The Hitchcock movie *The Birds* has given some folks a phobia about that, too.

UPPER GRAND COULEE

Columnar basalt

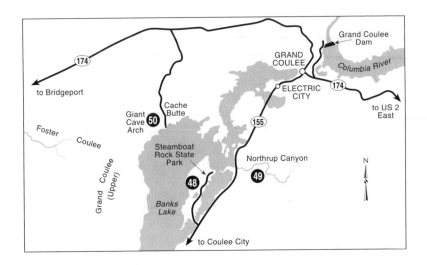

48 STEAMBOAT ROCK

Length: round trip 2 to 3 miles
High point: 2285 feet
Elevation gain: (on return) 525 feet
Management: Steamboat Rock State Park
USGS maps: Steamboat Rock S.W., Steamboat Rock S.E., Electric City, Barker Canyon

Steamboat Prow, on Mount Rainier, is called that because the wedge of rock has the look of a vessel pushing up through the mass of ice flowing down from Columbia Crest. Steamboat Rock gets its name even more aptly, because it once was truly an island in the middle of a mighty river, and though the mass of rock withstood the most horrendous floods of which geologists have found evidence in all the history of the earth, its streamlined shape, the prow pointing upstream, does indeed remind, say, of the steamboats Mark Twain used to pilot down and up the Mississippi. Left high and dry when the floods ceased, the resemblance to a steamboat has been revived by the engineers who drowned the floor of the Grand Coulee for irrigation and hydroelectric purposes, so that the onetime island is bounded on three sides by the water of Banks Lake (Equalizing Reservoir). The upstream end of the island (now peninsula) is in Steamboat Rock State Park.

Drive SR 155 north of US 2 and south of Grand Coulee Dam to Steamboat Rock State Park. The trailhead is opposite the entry to the

Air view of Steamboat Rock and Banks Reservoir

second campground (sites 51 to 105), elevation 1760 feet. No parking space here, so proceed to the picnic area.

The trail takes dead aim on Steamboat Rock, clambers through the one and only opening in the 300-foot cliffs, and in 1 mile from the car attains the nearly flat summit, 2285 feet. A path of sorts circles the plateau. Views are superb up and down the Grand Coulee, over Banks Reservoir to lava ramparts. The knowing eye can read millions of years of history: the Age of Fire when lava periodically flowed over what is now the Columbia Plateau, piling one layer atop the other; in

147

Granite boulder, a glacier erratic on top of Steamboat Rock

"modern times" the Age of Ice, when the continental ice sheet trundled down from Canada. The latter episode is dramatically recalled by a large granite boulder perched atop the lava, its light color atop the dark basalt standing out like a sore thumb. Did a lobe of Pleistocene ice thrust to this point, dropping the Canadian rock, a "glacial erratic"? The job could as readily have been done when the ice dam of Lake Missoula busted and the floodwaters scoured out the Channeled Scablands and gouged the Grand Coulee. An iceberg could have ridden the torrent, dumping its load here.

Flowers? Oh yes, abundant in season. Birds? Also, here and in the adjoining Banks Lake Wildlife Recreation Area. The geology, though, is the star.

49 NORTHRUP CANYON AND WAGON ROAD

Length: round trip canyon 3 miles; wagon road 3 miles
High point: canyon 2300 feet (approximate); wagon road 2400 feet (approximate)
Elevation gain: canyon 600 feet (approximate); wagon road 500 feet (approximate)
Management: Steamboat Rock State Park
USGS maps: Steamboat Rock S.W., Electric City

Northrup Canyon is a transition zone—geologically, ecologically, and historically. Basalt lies on granite that predates the lava flows. Sagebrush-steppe interfingers with forests of fir and pine. Desiccated buildings of a nineteenth-century homestead totter vacantly near the tidy dwelling of a park ranger.

Drive SR 155 to Steamboat Rock State Park Rest Area and boat ramp, near milepost 19, (don't be confused by the campground road to the south), and turn uphill on a gravel road 0.7 mile to a gate, the entrance to Northrup Canyon Natural Area. Park here, elevation 1800 feet.

Walk the road beyond the gate some 2 miles, passing an enormous heap of rusted tin cans (a 1930s dump by construction camps during the building of Grand Coulee Dam), the shade of piney-woods, farm fields, and a creek, to an old log barn built in 1889—and a Steamboat Rock State Park house. Elevation, 1850 feet. Proceed left, past an old chicken house, and find a good trail, which, with many steep ups and downs considerably in forest shadows, climbs a (net) 300 feet in 1½ miles to Northrup Lake, elevation 2134 feet. In 1 more mile the trail climbs another 200 feet out of the canyon to the lone prairie, bury me not.

A second walk from the same trailhead, along the old Northrup Canyon Wagon Road, has very special historical interest. In an era when giant machines powered by petroleum move mountains, the traveler over wildlands and through time cannot but be bemused by meager scratches in the terrain made solely by musclepower for wheels moved by actual (and very little) horsepower. The effort that went into it tells that this scratch once was a socially important route, ascending from

Barn built in 1889 on homestead in Northrup Canyon

Asters

Grand Coulee via Northrup Canyon to the sagebrush plateau. The old road was part of the stagecoach route from Almira that descended Northrup Canyon, crossed the dry floor of what is now Banks Reservoir, and ascended Barker Canyon to Brewster and Bridgeport. Important no longer to the Gross National Product and impassable even to wagons, it yet serves human feet very decently, and the human spirit too, providing a link to the very recent human past.

At the entry of Northrup Canyon Natural Area go right from the gate, beside the fence, and in 100 feet find the wagon road where it enters the woods. The way climbs steadily, soon leaving the trees to cross a large rockslide. Pause to visualize the picks, the shovels, the sweaty brows, the aching backs that forced a wheel track through the rocks. In a scant 1 mile the road is brushed in; trail diverges and continues, climbing sagebrush to a knoll. Explore onward over a series of knolls with views down Northrup Canyon. Alternately, climb another 150 feet, avoiding the fence marking the boundary of private land, and from the canyon rim look down and west to Banks Reservoir.

GIANT CAVE ARCH

Length: round trip 1 to 2 miles
High point: 2000 feet (approximate)
Elevation gain: 300 feet (approximate)
Management: State Wildlife Department
USGS map: Barker Canyon

The small cave shelters in the lower Grand Coulee generally have flat floors and a lived-in look. The floor of this large cave, on the canyon wall west of Banks Lake, slopes away, giving an archlike appearance.

Drive SR 174, the highway from Grand Coulee Dam to Bridgeport.

Between mileposts 11 and 12 turn south on graveled Barker Canyon Road, once a link in the Brewster–Bridgeport–Almira Stagecoach Road (see Hike 49). In 5.8 miles, at a four-way junction, go right on a dirt track until it becomes too rough. Elevation, 1700 feet.

The cave is in plain view high on the cliff to the south. A straight line seems the easiest approach, but a hill lies in the way and a circular route is better. Walk towards the cave. About 200 feet from the track-end, go left on a well-defined trail headed south gaining elevation. A bit beyond the arch find a lesser-used trail to a mountain-size heap of rock directly below the cave. Pick the best available way up the cobbles to the cave, elevation 2000 feet.

Giant Arch Cave (top center)

The cave is so big and its flat space so limited, a person must wonder if folks ever sought shelter here in ancient times. However, artifacts prove it has had some use in modern times. Ancient artifacts are protected by law, but not modern artifacts; feel free to pack out empty, discarded beer cans.

If you have time on your hands and vigor in your feet, return to the trail and follow it south an up-and-down 1 mile to cliffs below Foster Coulee. The route is ended by basalt walls edging Banks Reservoir.

51 HAWK BAY

Length: round trip 1 to 2 miles
High point: 1370 feet (approximate)
Elevation gain: 70 feet (approximate)
Management: Coulee Dam National Recreation Area
USGS map: Olsen Canyon

The south shore of Franklin D. Roosevelt Lake (reservoir) is excellent sagebrush country with magnificent reservoir views thrown in. Unfortunately, most of the narrow strip of public land along the shore is cut off from roads by private property and is accessible only by boat.

The one exception is Hawk Bay, tucked away in the eastern end of Lake Roosevelt—the flooded canyon where Hawk Creek once flowed into the Spokane River and thence into the Columbia. Besides the usual steppe flowers, there are a bit of scenic grandeur, a waterfall, and sandy beaches for sunbathing and swimming. Come here when the reservoir is full. When the water is down beautiful Hawk Bay is a mud flat.

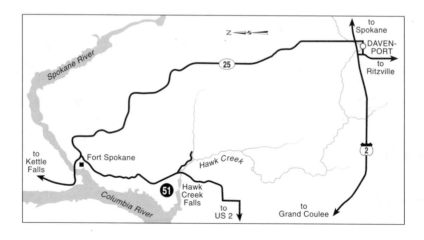

Hawk Bay

Drive US 2 either east to Davenport or west to Creston. From Davenport, go north on SR 25. Just 0.5 mile short of Fort Spokane, go left 6.2 miles on a road signed "Seven Bays Marina" and proceed to Hawk Creek Campground. From Creston, continue on US 2 for 2 miles and near milepost 232 go left 11.8 miles on the county road signed "Lake Roosevelt" and "Fort Spokane 18." At 3.2 miles pass Lincoln Road; at 8 miles cross Hawk Creek and turn left into Hawk Creek Campground, elevation 1300 feet.

If not staying at the campground, park near the boat ramp and walk either a narrow trail or a gated road, climbing a low hump to a view out to Roosevelt Lake. Beyond the fences one can climb open hillsides for a wide view of the lake or walk the lakeshore trail as far as it goes.

No fences or boundary markers show where public and private land meet. The shore is all public, as is most of the high hill overlooking the reservoir.

The waterfall and the hundred or more cliff swallows nesting at the upper end of the campground are worth the short walk.

NORTHERN STATE

Campbell Lake

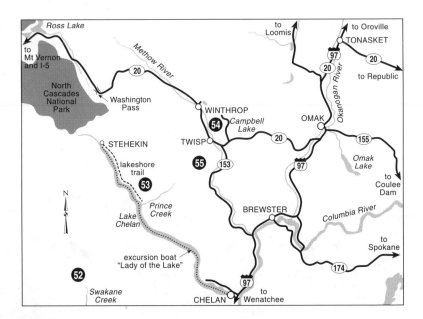

52   LEWISIA TWEEDYI

The stunningly beautiful flower is the subject here, the site incidental. The species is threatened, not endangered, and not really rare, just rarely seen in a very limited locality, and uncommon enough it has no common name. Like its cousin, *Lewisia rediviva* (bitterroot), it blooms but briefly. The plant is protected by law so take only pictures. It is also protected by a conspiracy to keep secrets. However, two places to find the plant are known so widely they may be described here to make it new friends—which means defenders.

The easiest to drive to but hardest to hike is road No. 7903 in Tumwater Canyon. The easiest walking and most difficult driving is the Swakane Canyon road.

Tumwater Botanical Area

Length: round trip ½ to 8 miles
High point: 3100 feet
Elevation gain: 100 to 1400 feet
Management: Wenatchee National Forest
USGS map: Winton

Drive US 2 between Tumwater Campground and Leavenworth. At 1.3 miles downstream from the Wenatchee River bridge, between

Lewisia tweedyi

mileposts 92 and 93, find road No. 7903 and park near the gate, elevation 1700 feet.

The footroad is steep, darn steep. Within a few hundred feet look for *Lewisia tweedyi* in rock outcrops on the hillside above the road. In 1 mile, pass road No. (7903)200. At 1½ miles reach sagebrush hillsides, elevation 2600 feet. At 3 miles go right and follow the ridge top to more open slopes and a 3100-foot high point.

Swakane Canyon

Length: round trip 4 or more miles
High point: 2600 feet
Elevation gain: 800 feet
Management: State Wildlife Department
USGS maps: Rocky Reach, Chumstick

Swakane Valley, typical of the Transition Zone of eastern Washington foothills, has forest on the valley floor, sagebrush on south-facing slopes, and forest on ridge tops. It has two other features less usual. In

1988 a fire swept through, scorching trees and killing some, greatly enlarging the sagebrush-steppe—except it also killed sagebrush. Not to worry. Fire is part of nature. Visitors will be edified on successive trips, observing the evolution of the landscape over the years, returning to its pre-fire condition. A second reason for the successive trips is that the valley is one of the few well-publicized places to be introduced to *Lewisia tweedyi.*

Drive US 97 north of Wenatchee. At milepost 205, 0.8 mile beyond Rocky Reach Dam (the dam, not the entrance road) go west on the graveled Swakane Valley road. In 1 mile enter the Swakane Wildlife Recreation Area. At 3 miles is a junction (unsigned in 1996). The Rattlesnake Spring road goes right, climbing very steeply 2300 feet through open steppe to forest on the ridge. The views and flowers are great but the walking is not. Better, go left from the junction until the road becomes too mean for the family car. A good stopping point is 4.5 miles from the highway, elevation 1800 feet.

The road enters forest, in 2 miles opening to steppe. But don't feel compelled to stick with the road. Climb the hillsides to the north—these face south and thus are wide open almost all the way to Rattlesnake Spring before yielding to forest.

53 CHELAN LAKESHORE TRAIL

Length: one way 18 miles
High point: 1700 feet
Elevation gain: gross gain 3000 feet; net gain 0
Management: Wenatchee National Forest and North Cascades National Park
USGS maps: Lucerne, Prince Creek, Sun Mountain, Stehekin

Lake Chelan, the 55-mile-long inland fjord whose upper shores lie in the Glacier Peak Wilderness, the Lake Chelan–Sawtooth Wilderness, and the Lake Chelan National Recreation Area, has been famed across the nation since it became, in 1968, the entry to the new North Cascades National Park. No road from outside intrudes on Stehekin, at the head of the lake; visitors come by boat, by airplane, and (the elect) on foot. A number of trails, snowfree and open to travel in summer, follow high lines over the mountains into the Stehekin valley. The classic route in spring is the low line along the lakeshore, beside waves stirred by cooling winds, on bluffs with breath-stopping views. The way goes from sagebrush-steppe into forests of ponderosa pine and Douglas fir and groves of aspen, emerges to pinegrass lawns atop rock buttresses, dips to slot gorges chilled by summer-long waterfalls. The flower show, which begins in late March and early April, features glacier lily, spring beauty, trillium, yellow bells, chocolate lily, and their usual companions. The procession continues through May into July. Spring gold, prairie star, blue-eyed Mary, naked broomrape,

Lake Chelan from the Lakeshore Trail

primrose monkeyflower, death camas, balsamroot, miners lettuce, calypso, onion, penstemon, serviceberry, suksdorfia, saxifrage, fairy bells, paintbrush, red currant, collomia, tiger lily, pussytoes, shooting star, and many more take their star turns.

The schedule of the passenger boats changes with the seasons; for current information call the NPS-USFS Information Center in Seattle. Do not come lacking a wad of cash money. The parking-lot fee at Field's Point is $4 a night, the round-trip boat ticket is $21, and everything for sale on the boat and in Stehekin is hugely costly.

Hikers customarily take the *Lady of the Lake,* more respectfully leisurely of the two boats, and board uplake at Field's Point. The *Lady* arrives there at 9:45 A.M. in the best hiking season, late spring, and at about 11:30 A.M. unloads boots at the Prince Creek Campground trailhead, elevation 1098 feet.

The hike strategy depends on available time and energy—and esthetic sensitivity. The 2-day fast track preferred by hurry-warts in a rush to get there so they can get home is 11 miles on debarkation afternoon and 7 miles the next morning, to catch the boat on its 2:00 P.M. departure downlake. The swifties can then check off the trip and jet to Everest, memory not cluttered with flowers because they went by in a blur, nor with rattlesnakes because they kept striking empty air three

Lake Chelan from Flick Creek Shelter

paces in the wake of the boots. As the surveyor has learned more flowers and gotten to know snakes and thus become a wiser and altogether better person, his personal itinerary has expanded to a minimum of 5 days, camping (actually merely rest-stopping overnight, leaving no trace; as the old saying from the Alps has it, "Though the food is cold, the inner man is hot") at irresistible spots the dasher and prancer never suspect. **Note:** Wood fires are banned within 1 mile of the shore except at official fire installations—Prince Creek, Meadow Creek Shelter, Moore Point, and Lakeshore Shelter.

An 11-mile afternoon can be cruel and inhuman when the sagebrush-steppe is radiating heat waves. Some parties therefore spend a first night at Prince Creek, eating the watermelon they have been clever enough to bring, and set out on the trail in the morning cool. Otherwise, by the most common schedule, the first night is spent at or near Meadow Creek Shelter, 7 miles, and the second night at Moore Point, 11 miles. The initial 7-mile afternoon is not life-threatening, and the short second day allows leisure to poke about the ancient orchard, New England–like stone fences, alien flowers and shrubs recalling gardens of old, and relicts of the hotel where Inland Empire gentry assembled at the turn of the century while across the lake at Lucerne the "dirty miners in search of shining gold" socialized with dirty girls. The third day has time enough before the *Lady* heads downlake to tour the National Park Service museum and nature trails; if a fourth day is wanted to see more of Stehekin, the Purple Point Campground is handy.

From Prince Creek's alluvial fan the trail ascends sagebrush, drops and climbs, dips in and out of deep wooded cools of Rattlesnake, Rex, Pioneer, and Cascade Creeks. The Meadow Creek Shelter is appealing in bad weather; in good, more attractive alternatives can be found throughout the black forest dating from 1985, when a group of Eastern backpackers burnt their toilet paper, as instructed in a manual by this surveyor, which is why he proudly commissioned installation of trail signs designating "Harvey's Burn." The forest badly needed the opening up previously denied by the fanaticism of that ecological ignoramus, Smokey the Bear.

The trail climbs from the burn to its high point of 1700 feet in a private "tree farm," which does little for the national economy or forest health but certainly defaces the wilderness. A steep drop ends at wild-thrashing Fish Creek. A side trail leads down the creek to the hotel site on Moore Point. The *Lady* stops here on request to drop off or pick up hikers; the Moore-to-Stehekin walk is a popular abbreviation of the full classic.

From the Fish Creek bridge the way is up again, to the climax views from Hunts Bluff, 1600 feet, another possible no-fire, carry-water "rest stop extended overnight" for the sake of the mystical experience. The trail plummets from bluff to lake, crosses more delicious creeks, passes Lakeshore Shelter, a delight of a camp on a rock peninsula but almost always occupied. The relentless up-and-down ceases as the route rounds cliffs and sidehills forest to Stehekin.

54   CAMPBELL LAKE

Length: round trip from Campbell Lake 1 mile; from upper parking lot 1 mile
High point: from lake 3100 feet; from upper parking lot 4000 feet
Elevation gain: from lake 300 feet; from upper parking lot 300 feet (on
    return)
Management: State Wildlife Department
USGS map: Twisp

Grand expanses of sky-open sagebrush, rolling meadows of wild-flowers, and, in early spring, hundreds of migrating deer make the Methow Wildlife Recreation Area a hiker's joy. The blossoming is several weeks later up here than in the valley bottoms; from low elevation to high the springtime is months long.

Drive SR 20 east to Winthrop or Twisp, follow Airport Road on the north side of the Methow River 1.8 miles from Winthrop or 7.2 miles from Twisp and turn uphill on the Bear Creek road, signed "Campbell

Shrub-steppe above Campbell Lake

Lake 6 miles." At 1.8 miles from Airport Road go right on a dirt road signed "Campbell Lake 4 miles" and enter the Methow Wildlife Recreation Area. Climb steeply from forest to meadow. At 1.2 miles from the Bear Creek road keep right. In another 1.2 miles is another junction (unsigned in 1996). The right fork goes in 1 mile to Campbell Lake and Pipestone Canyon. Park near the lake, elevation 2800 feet, and climb the hill to the south.

The left fork climbs a long mile to a large parking area, elevation 3200 feet. The road continues but it's time to walk. To the south is a small knoll with a large view. Beyond stretch miles of meadow; across the Methow Valley the horizon is dominated by Mount Gardner and Silver Star. Descend the ridge ½ mile to a promontory with an even better view of the valley, plus a look down the awesome cliffs of Pipestone Canyon, famous for rattlesnakes.

Campbell Lake

55 SMITH CANYON

Length: round trip: to ridge 3 miles; to Lookout Mountain 7 miles
High point: ridge 4000 feet; Lookout Mountain 5515 feet
Elevation gain: to ridge 1300 feet; to Lookout Mountain 2815 feet
Management: Okanogan National Forest
USGS map: Twisp

Smith Canyon is a textbook example of the East Cascades transition downward from highland forest to sagebrush-steppe. Shaded north slopes have trees; sun-open south slopes are flower-meadowed in late April with balsamroot (sunflowers), blue lupine and mertensia, and the highly edible miner's lettuce.

From SR 153 between Pateros and Twisp, between mileposts 21 and 22 (1.2 miles south of Carlton), turn uphill on the paved Libby Creek road signed "Blackpine Lake." In 2.5 miles (from the highway) go right on a road signed "Chicamun Canyon." At 3.7 miles go right on

Arrow-leaf balsamroot

an unmarked road. At 5.5 miles from the highway, just short of a ranch gate, turn right again on road No. (4342)100 and drive a final 0.4 mile to a gate, closed during the deer-migrating season and a good place to park any time of the year, elevation 2700 feet.

Walk through timber a scant $\frac{1}{2}$ mile to a meadow overlooking the ranch. A very nice wandering is up the hill from here but the better choices are another $\frac{3}{4}$ mile, at a stream crossing. The right side offers a fine walk, mostly on animal traces, to a 4000-foot ridge; views toward Twisp are blocked by trees but snowy summits of the Sawtooth Range are close. On the left side of the creek an easy route leads to the top of 5515-foot Lookout Mountain and a fire lookout with all-around-the-compass views of the Methow Valley and Cascades.

APPENDIX: SAGEBRUSH COUNTRY

Franklin and Dyrness (see below) define three major types of steppe. What they call *shrub-steppe* dominates the walking routes described in this book. Taylor and Valum (also below) prefer *sagebrush-steppe,* though they acknowledge that a number of shrubs resemble and are frequently mistaken for the big (tall) sagebrush, which is "the most widespread, most common, most ecologically important" plant. Whatever the name, it is by no means a monotonously uniform scene. Mastroguiseppe and Gill (below) list the diverse habitats as "deep sandy loams, iron-oxide rich; non-iron-oxide-rich lithosols; talus slopes; cliffs; springs; washes; riparian fringes; alkaline areas; river floodbars; alluvial fans; deposits of volcanic tuff; seeps and springs; drifting sand." Taylor and Valum describe in some detail the mosaic of the sagebrush (shrub)-steppe:

"Standard-Type" Zone: Sandy-gravelly soil. Dominated by big sagebrush and grasses. However, near forest margins, the sagebrush is replaced by bitterbrush and in drier areas by rabbitbrush, both of which often are mistaken for sagebrush. Notable flowers include buckwheat, paintbrush, lupine, balsamroot, larkspur, phlox, desert parsley, locoweed, daisy, onion, death camas, and brodiea.

Lithosol Zone: The term means "rock soil" or "stone soil"; within the coverage of this book the rock is most commonly basalt. (Deposits of St. Helens ash from the eruption of 1980 are widespread.) This is the "desert-alpine" zone that looks so much like the fellfields (rock fields) of arctic-alpine tundra. The plants are low-growing, resembling cushion plants of the tundra. Notable flowers include rock sagebrush, buckwheat, dwarf goldenweed, phlox, rock penstemon, daisy, and (spectacularly) bitterroot and both of Washington's cacti.

Sand Dune Zone: Notable flowers include sand dock, dune primrose, and dune monkeyflower.

Talus Zone: Serviceberry and squaw currant form thickets. Notable flowers include purple sage, Oregon sunshine, penstemon, buckwheat, and evening primrose.

Saline Zone: Notable plants of the "salt pans" include hop sage, winter fat, and greasewood.

Meadow Zone: More strictly, "wet meadow" or "wetland." Depressions may be wet enough (normally in spring, only) to form meadows characterized by sedge, rush, iris, willow, and camas.

Seepage Areas: Subsurface water oozing or dribbling from lava strata nourishes brilliant rock gardens of monkeyflower, shooting star, and saxifrage.

Riparian Areas: On floodplains beside streams are lush fields of sod-forming grasses, rich in herbs, with an abundance of shrubs such as serviceberry, creek dogwood, and bitter cherry, as well as groves of aspen, cottonwood, and willow and stands of ponderosa pine.

Plants to Notice

A few specific notes drawn from Taylor and Valum, Hitchcock and Cronquist, and other sources noted below may be given as introduction to those volumes.

"The single most important group of plants is in the Grass Family: spiked wheatgrass, steppe bluegrass, Idaho fescue, cheat grass, Indian rice grass, needle grass, giant wild rye, etc." A great many of the grasses now common in the steppe were not here a century ago, before the advance of the grazing frontier. Cheat grass is a notorious alien weed. The walker who learns to distinguish the invaders from the natives is able to identify pristine (mainly) and disturbed (largely) steppe.

The Composite (Aster, Sunflower) Family has scores of "daisies," "sunflowers," and "dandelions," most of which are something else. The supremely outstanding genus of the steppe is the *Artemisia,* containing the sagebrushes, mugworts, and wormwoods. Species of *Artemisia* are virtually the only ones that are metabolically active most of the year. *A. tridentata* (big, or tall, sagebrush) is the superstar, growing from 1 to 8 feet tall, ranging upward to the cold timberline; it has a characteristic strong odor; leaves are distinctively three-lobed. *A. rigida* (stiff sagebrush) occurs in the lithosol, growing as tall as 2 feet; leaves are deeply divided rather than lobed. *A. arbuscula* is a low, dwarf sagebrush. *A. norvegica* is mountain sagebrush. *A. frigida* is pasture sagebrush or prairie sagewort. And so on and so on; there are many other common *Artemisia* species. In the same family but another genus is *Chrysothamaus nauseosus,* common, or gray, rabbitbrush, often taken for a sagebrush, as noted above.

Bitterbrush is even more often mistaken for a sagebrush, partly because like the *A. tridentata* it has three-lobed leaves. In fact, it's in the Rose Family, as is yclept *Purshia tridentata.* Other prominent members of the family are serviceberry, cinquefoil, old man's beard—and roses.

The sage so beloved in legend and song and nose, the purple sage (or grayball), is *Salvia dorrii* of the Mint Family. A sniff tells you that.

A shrub demanding a special spotlight is *Ceanothus velutinus,* the snowbrush, in the Buckthorn Family. It thrives at the upper edge of steppe, amid the pinegrass slopes of the ponderosa pine forest. The delicate perfume of the flowers is pleasing to the nose. In the heat of the day the foliage emits creosote-like vapors, the "Ceanothus reek," which is the most characteristic aroma of the East Side above the sage; West-Siders typically begin by detesting the reek, end by loving it for the connotations of sunshine and flowers.

Among other visually prominent shrubs are squaw currant, in the Currant Family, and mock orange, in the Syringa Family.

A person can scarcely travel the steppe without "tumbling along with the tumbling tumbleweed." The Goosefoot Family offers a Eurasian weed, *Salsola kali,* the Russian thistle, or wind witch. In the Amaranth Family is *Amaranthus albus,* the white pigweed. Nor can we omit, in the Mustard Family, *Sisymbrium altissimum,* the tumbling (Jim Hill) mustard.

Though a West-Sider cannot believe it until he sees it, the Cactus Family embellishes Washington (most especially in the lithosol steppe) with *Opuntia polyacantha,* the prickly pear, the blossoms lemon-yellow to peach, and *Pediocactus simpsonii,* the hedgehog, flowering rose-purple-yellow.

Moving swiftly along in highlights: Lily Family—onion, brodiea, camas, death camas, yellow bell, Mariposa lily; Iris Family—iris, grass widow; Buckwheat Family—buckwheats!; Purslane Family—bitterroot, spring beauty; Pink Family—sandwort; Buttercup Family—buttercup, larkspur; Mustard Family—rock cress, wallflower, bee plant; Stonecrop Family—stonecrop; Saxifrage Family—prairie star, alumroot, saxifrage; Pea Family—locoweed, lupine, vetch, large-headed clover; Geranium Family—sticky geranium; Evening Primrose Family—clarkia; Parsley Family—desert parsley; Primrose Family—shooting star; Phlox Family—phlox, collomia; Waterleaf Family—phacelia, ballhead waterleaf; Borage Family—mertensia, fiddleneck; Figwort Family—penstemon, paintbrush, monkeyflower.

That's for openers.

For Further Information

Two outstanding "schools" are held each year, the faculties composed of professors, academic and lay; students welcome at every level from primary to advanced; the tuition free.

Annually since 1953, Memorial Day weekend has been the date of the Audubon Campout, attended by members from throughout the region, the public warmly invited. For details see Hike 25, Audubon Camp, then call your local Audubon chapter.

In mid-May (usually) the Washington Native Plant Society offers a similar campout—a Spring Study Weekend—in the transition zone between steppe and forest. Though the event is for members, that's easy—annual dues are only $12 ($15 family, $8 student or retiree). And with a membership a person receives the quarterly *Douglasia,* the statewide journal, plus monthly bulletins of chapters sited around the state, as well as the Occasional Papers published from time to time. Each chapter has a regular schedule of walks and hikes where the novice may sit at the feet or dog the heels of experts ever willing to identify species. For information write Peggy Butler, Washington Native Plant Society, 2811 Langridge Loop NW, Olympia, WA 98502.

Following are the books the authors have consulted:

Sagebrush Country, Ronald J. Taylor and Rolf W. Valum, Mountain Press Publishing Co., P.O. Box 2399, Missoula, MT 59801, 1992. Dozens of flowers in color photographs, habitat descriptions, and evocations of "a fantasy land rich in legend . . ." and of "camping under the stars with the ever-present smell of sage, listening for the eerie howl of the ubiquitous coyote, and being keenly aware of the 'aloneness' so closely associated with the wide open spaces. . . ."

Natural Vegetation of Oregon and Washington, Jerry F. Franklin and C. T. Dyrness, U.S. Forest Service, Portland, Oregon, 1973. Reissued in 1989 with a bibliographic supplement by Oregon State University Press, Corvallis, Oregon. A comprehensive and definitive description of the region's vegetation areas, their physical characteristics and plant communities, from the Pacific Ocean to Idaho, British Columbia to California, sea level to glacier level. The basic manual of the scientist, yet with language, photographs, maps, and charts that make it readily accessible to the lay reader.

Flora of the Pacific Northwest, C. Leo Hitchcock and Arthur Cronquist, University of Washington Press, Seattle, 1973. The "Big Book" condensed to a single weighty volume, as much as the ordinary hiker can carry in his pack; the five-volume version is better but requires five hikers.

Steppe by Step: Understanding Priest Rapids Plants, Joy D. Mastroguiseppe and Steven J. Gill, Douglasia Occasional Papers, Washington Native Plant Society, 1983. The habitats at Priest Rapids on the Columbia River include most of those found on the steppe. This close examination of a single richly diverse site is relevant throughout the area.

Plant Life of the North Cascades, Douglasia Occasional Papers, Washington Native Plant Society, 1986. Covers the habitats of the high alpine area and down through the transition zones to the steppe of Lake Chelan.

Land Above the Trees, Ann H. Zwinger and Beatrice E. Willard, Harper and Row, New York, 1972. This "Guide to American Alpine Tundra" says much about the lands above the cold timberline that applies to the lands below the dry timberline.

Timberline, Stephen F. Arno and Ramona P. Hammerly, The Mountaineers, Seattle, 1984. The emphasis is the cold timberline but something also is said about the dry timberline.

The authors would like to express thanks for counsel graciously provided by Jerry F. Franklin, of the U.S. Forest Service and the University of Washington College of Forest Resources, and Arthur R. Kruckeberg, of the University of Washington Department of Botany and founder of the Washington Native Plant Society.

The Land Managers

For up-to-date information on road conditions and when wildflowers will be at their best, contact the land managers. Individual wildlife recreation areas and state parks do not maintain office staffs, so phone their regional offices.

DEPARTMENT OF WILDLIFE
Region No. 1: North 8702 Division Street, Spokane, WA 99218; phone (509) 456-4082

Hike 7   Tucannon River

Region No. 2: 1540 Alder Street Northwest, Ephrata, WA 98823; phone (509) 754-4624

Hike 28   Winchester Wasteway
Hike 29   Potholes Island Hideaway (or Desert Islands)
Hike 33   Goose Lakes Plateau
Hike 36   Ancient Lakes
Hike 37   Dusty Lake
Hike 38   Frenchman Coulee
Hike 42   East Saddle Mountain
Hike 50   Giant Cave Arch
Hike 54   Campbell Lake

Region No. 3: 2802 Fruitvale Boulevard, Yakima, WA 98902; phone (509) 575-2740

Hike 18   Naches River–Cougar Canyon
Hike 19   Cleman Mountain
Hike 20   Yakima River View
Hike 21   Umtanum Canyon
Hike 22   Yakima Rim Skyline Trail
Hike 23   Hardy Canyon
Hike 24   Black Canyon–Umtanum Ridge Crest
Hike 25   Audubon Camp
Hike 26   Manastash Ridge
Hike 27   West Manastash Ridge
Hike 34   Colockum Wildlife Recreation Area
Hike 35   Colockum Pass Road
Hike 40   Whiskey Dick Mountain

WASHINGTON STATE PARKS
Region No. 3: 2201 North Duncan Drive, Wenatchee, WA 98801; phone (509) 662-0420

Hike 1   Swale Canyon
Hike 39   Trees of Stone
Hike 43   Summer Falls
Hike 44   The Grand Coulee–Lenore Lake Cave Shelters
Hike 45   Coulee City Stagecoach Road–Deep Lake
Hike 46   Monument Coulee
Hike 47   Dry Falls Cave
Hike 48   Steamboat Rock
Hike 49   Northrup Canyon and Wagon Road

Region No. 4: Route 9, Box 251, Sacajawea Park Road, Pasco, WA 99358; phone (509) 545-2315

Hike 3   Horsethief Lake State Park—She-Who-Watches
Hike 4   Crow Butte
Hike 8   Chief Old Bones
Hike 9   Palouse Falls

WENATCHEE AND OKANOGAN NATIONAL FORESTS
Naches Ranger District: 510 Highway 12, Naches, WA 98937; phone (509) 653-2205

Hike 15   Conrad Meadows
Hike 17   Bear Canyon

Chelan Ranger District: 428 West Woodin Avenue, Chelan, WA 98816; phone (509) 682-2576

Hike 53   Chelan Lakeshore Trail

Twisp Ranger District: P.O. Box 188, Twisp, WA 98856; phone (509) 997-2131

Hike 54   Campbell Lake
Hike 55   Smith Canyon

COLUMBIA NATIONAL WILDLIFE AREA
U.S. Fish & Wildlife Service: Othello, WA 99344; phone (509) 489-2668

Hike 30   Blythe Lake and Coulee
Hike 31   Potholes Canal
Hike 32   Crab Creek Trails

COULEE DAM NATIONAL RECREATION AREA
National Park Service: Box 37, Coulee Dam, WA 99116; phone (509) 633-0881

Hike 51   Hawk Bay

INDEX

Ancient Lake (Hike 36) 11, 14, 123
Audubon Camp 98

Babcock Bench 127
Bald Mountain 76
Banks Lake 146
Bear Canyon 71
Benge 55
Billy Clapp Reservoir 136
Birdsong Camp 89
Black Canyon 96
Blue Slide Lookout 63
Blythe Lake 110

Campbell Lake (Hike 54) 155, 162
Chelan Lakeshore Trail 158
Cherry Orchard Trail 38
Chief Old Bones 50
Cleman Mountain 75
Colockum Pass Road 122
Colockum Wildlife Recreation
  Area 119, 122
Columbia National Wildlife
  Refuge 105, 110, 112, 114, 117
Columbia River 38, 39, 42, 45, 50,
  127, 131
Conrad Meadows (Hike 15) 57, 68
Cougar Canyon 73
Coulee City Stagecoach Road 140
Cowiche Canyon Conservancy 70
Crab Creek 112, 114, 115
Crow Butte 42

Dalles Mountain Ranch 41
Darland Mountain 61
Darling Mountain 61
Deep Lake (Hike 45) 2, 140
Devils Canyon 54
Dry Falls Cave 143
Dry Falls Lake 143
Dusty Lake 125

Field's Point 160
Folsom Lake 56
Franklin D. Roosevelt Lake 152
Frenchman Coulee (Hike 38) 126
Frog Lake 115

Giant Cave Arch 150
Ginkgo Petrified Forest State
  Park 128
Goose Lakes Plateau 117
Grand Coulee 138
Green Lake 143

Hardy Canyon (Hike 23) 93, 94
Hawk Bay 152
Horsethief Butte 41
Horsethief Lake State Park 39

Jacob Durr Road 82
Juniper Dunes Wilderness 46

Kahlotus 54
Klickitat River 36

L. T. Murray Wildlife Recreation
  Area 81
Lenore Lake Cave Shelters 138
Long Lake Wildlife Recreation
  Area 136
Lookout Mountain 164
Lyle-to-Goldendale Rails-to-
  Trails 36
Lyons Ferry State Park 50

Manastash Ridge 98, 100
Marsh Loop Trail 116
Meadow Creek Shelter 161
Methow Wildlife Recreation
  Area 162
Monument Coulee 142
Moore Point 161

Index

Naches River 73
Narrow Neck Gap 66
North Cascade National Park 158
Northrup Canyon Natural
Area 148
Northrup Canyon 148
Northrup Lake (Hike 49) 17

Oak Creek Wildlife Recreation
Area 74
Okanogan National Forest 163

Palouse Falls 51
Pasco–Fish Lake–Spokane Rails-
to-Trails 53
Potholes Reservoir 108
Potholes Canal 112
Prince Creek 160
Purple Point Campground 161

Quilomene Wildlife Recreation
Area 120, 131
Quincy Wildlife Recreation Area
123, 125, 126

Red Alkali Lake 143
Roza Creek 88
Roza Dam 82, 88

Saddle Mountain 133
Sedge Ridge 58
Seeps Lakes Wildlife Recreation
Area 114, 117
She-Who-Watches 39, 40
Smith Canyon 163
Snake River 53
Steamboat Rock 146
Steamboat Rock State
Park 146, 148
Stehekin 161

Stratford Wildlife Recreation
Area 136
Summer Falls (Hike 43) 19, 136
Summer Falls State Park 136
Sun Lake State Park 140, 142
Swakane Canyon, 157
Swale Canyon 36

Trees of Stone 128
Tucannon Wildlife Recreation
Area (Hike 7) 16, 34, 48
Tucannon River 48
Tumwater Botanical Area 156
Tumwater Canyon 156
Turnbull National Wildlife
Refuge 56
Two Sisters Rocks (Hike 5)
35, 44

Umtanum Canyon 80
Umtanum Creek Recreation Area
78, 81
Umtanum Ridge Crest 96
University of Washington Obser-
vatory 102

W. T. Wooten Environmental
Center 49
Wanapum Breaks 131
Wanapum Lake 126
Wenatchee National Forest 158
West Manastash Ridge 102
Whiskey Dick Mountain 130
Winchester Wasteway 106

Yakima Skyline Rim Trail (Hike
22) 77, 81
Yakima River View 78
Yakima River 77

ABOUT THE AUTHORS

IRA SPRING is known nationwide as half of an outdoor photography team—Bob and Ira Spring—whose work has appeared in numerous national magazines and more than 50 books. While Bob has come to specialize in travel subjects, Ira delights in capturing outdoor and wildlife scenes wherever they occur. When he's not off taking pictures in places as far apart as the Pacific Northwest and the Alps, Ira hangs up his backpack in Edmonds, Washington.

HARVEY MANNING is one of the Pacific Northwest's most influential and outspoken conservationists. His preservation efforts have ranged from protection of the "Issaquah Alps" wilderness near his home in the Puget Sound region to helping attain national park status for the North Cascades. He and Ira Spring have introduced legions of future environmentalists to the Northwest wilderness with their *100 Hikes in*™ guidebooks, which include *100 Hikes in Washington's Alpine Lakes* and *100 Hikes in Washington's North Cascades National Park Region.*

Other titles you may enjoy from The Mountaineers:

100 HIKES IN WASHINGTON'S GLACIER PEAK REGION: THE NORTH CASCADES, 2nd Ed., *Ira Spring & Harvey Manning*

100 HIKES IN WASHINGTON'S NORTH CASCADES NATIONAL PARK REGION, 2nd Ed., *Ira Spring & Harvey Manning*

100 HIKES IN WASHINGTON'S SOUTH CASCADES AND OLYMPICS, 2nd Ed., *Ira Spring & Harvey Manning*

100 HIKES IN WASHINGTON'S ALPINE LAKES, 2nd Ed., *Ira Spring & Harvey Manning*

IMPRESSIONS OF THE NORTH CASCADES: Essays about a Northwest Landscape, *John C. Miles, editor*
A diverse collection of original essays explores Washington's North Cascades to create a unique portrait of a changing landscape.

EXPLORING WASHINGTON'S WILD AREAS: A Guide for Hikers, Backpackers, Climbers, X-C Skiers, & Paddlers, *Marge & Ted Mueller*
Guide to 55 wilderness areas with outstanding recreational opportunities, plus notes on history, geology, plants and animals, and wildlife.

HIKING THE MOUNTAINS TO SOUND GREENWAY, *Harvey Manning*
Recreational walks and all-day hikes along Puget Sound's I-90 corridor. Includes the history, founding, and future of the Greenway project.

OLYMPIC MOUNTAINS TRAIL GUIDE, 2nd Ed., *Robert L. Wood*
Revised guide to every trail in the Olympics, including scenic and historic highlights, mileages, and elevations.

THE IRON GOAT TRAIL, 2nd Ed., *Volunteers for Outdoor Washington, USDA Forest Service, & Mount Baker-Snoqualmie National Forest*
History-filled walking guide to the first railroad route across the Cascades.

THE MOUNTAINEERS, founded in 1906, is a nonprofit outdoor activity and conservation club, whose mission is "to explore, study, preserve, and enjoy the natural beauty of the outdoors. . . ." Based in Seattle, Washington, the club is now the third-largest such organization in the United States, with 15,000 members and five branches throughout Washington State.

The Mountaineers sponsors both classes and year-round outdoor activities in the Pacific Northwest, which include hiking, mountain climbing, ski-touring, snowshoeing, bicycling, camping, kayaking and canoeing, nature study, sailing, and adventure travel. The club's conservation division supports environmental causes through educational activities, sponsoring legislation, and presenting informational programs. All club activities are led by skilled, experienced volunteers, who are dedicated to promoting safe and responsible enjoyment and preservation of the outdoors.

If you would like to participate in these organized outdoor activities or the club's programs, consider a membership in The Mountaineers. For information and an application, write or call The Mountaineers, Club Headquarters, 300 Third Avenue West, Seattle, WA 98119; (206) 284-6310.

The Mountaineers Books, an active, nonprofit publishing program of the club, produces guidebooks, instructional texts, historical works, natural history guides, and works on environmental conservation. All books produced by The Mountaineers are aimed at fulfilling the club's mission.

Send or call for our catalog of more than 300 outdoor titles:

The Mountaineers Books
1001 SW Klickitat Way, Suite 201
Seattle, WA 98134
1-800-553-4453 / e-mail: mbooks@mountaineersbooks.org